I0517861

Praise for
Any Body Can Heal

"A powerful memoir about turmoil and growth, *Any Body Can Heal* celebrates the human spirit and what it can overcome."
—*Foreword* Clarion Reviews

"*Any Body Can Heal* is a powerful story of the body and mind's ability to protect and heal after traumatic events. Sara's raw honesty and her unyielding search for knowledge and understanding created a book that will help everyone who has suffered trauma."
—Jayna Hefford, five-time Olympian, honored member of the Hockey Hall of Fame, and motivational keynote speaker

any body can heal

any body can heal

a memoir about facing down trauma

sara davidson

Copyright © 2025 by Sara Davidson

All rights reserved.

No part of this book may be reproduced, or stored in a retrieval system, or transmitted in any form or by any means, electronic, mechanical, photocopying, recording, or otherwise, without express written permission of the publisher.

This is a memoir, and the events and experiences detailed in it have been presented as the author currently remembers them, to the best of her ability. Some names and identifying details have been changed to protect the privacy of individuals.

Published by GFB™, Seattle
www.girlfridayproductions.com

Produced by Girl Friday Productions

Cover design: Emily Weigel
Production editorial: Kylee Hayes
Project management: Kristin Duran

Image credits: cover © Shutterstock/ma_i_vi; Shutterstock/Super Shanoom

ISBN (paperback): 978-1-964721-01-9
ISBN (ebook): 978-1-964721-02-6

Library of Congress Control Number 2024918741

First edition

For my loved ones, who never wavered. For my son, who, more than anything, carried me through. For my angel, who held us both when I could not. For all the survivors.

Contents

Foreword

When trauma suddenly and hideously levelled Sara Davidson's life, she had no reason to believe she would ever recover. But rather than surrender to despair, she focused on rebuilding her life and reclaiming her authentic self. She already knew from her years as a semiprofessional athlete that pursuing a high-level goal requires determination, rigorous daily practice and commitment to an arduous, incremental process with highs and lows, gains and setbacks.

Sara's quest to understand her body's responses to trauma was often fraught with stress and anxiety. But what is so compelling about her story is that as she reveals *what* happened to her, and how her body responded to those events, she is less interested in what she endured than in understanding *why* her body responded to her trauma as it did. For Sara, knowing the what *and* the why gave her the tools she needed to understand *how* to heal her body and soul. And then, in her beautiful, generous way, she wrote a book to share what she learned with others who could benefit from the knowledge she'd gained.

Reading her story, I was struck by her courage, persistence and refusal to settle for anything less than reclaiming her true self and all the elements that constitute a joyful, meaningful life for her. Even more striking was her determination to acknowledge chaotic, often deeply uncomfortable feelings of doubt, fear, shame, frustration and rage. She teaches us that acknowledging difficult feelings is the first step towards strength and healing, and her book functions as a how-to guide of sorts for acknowledging and normalizing such feelings.

She didn't make it to the other side alone, of course. For as much as *Any Body Can Heal* is a story about the power of the human spirit to triumph over adversity, it is also a story about how much you need the support of a community to succeed in that endeavour.

Reading Sara's story, I was reminded of the concept of Ah Nee Na, which is central to the beliefs of the Squamish Nation, part of the Coast Salish Indigenous people of British Columbia. Ah Nee Na doesn't just speak to the power of individual resilience. It reinforces the idea that personal and communal well-being are deeply intertwined and it's important to maintain balance and harmony within oneself and with the broader community and environment because it is the collective support of the community that helps everyone within it rise and thrive.

A Squamish Nation elder once explained to me that Ah Nee Na is a type of Coast Salish blessing, both a comment and a wish that when you rise from a fall, your spirit self will rise along with your physical self. "Sometimes rising from a fall is easy," he said. But sometimes in order to get up and keep your spirit moving, you need help from those around you. Sara spent her formative years in Vancouver, BC. After reading *Any Body Can Heal*, I can't help but think that the concept of Ah Nee Na is baked into her being, for she is the first to acknowledge that her story might have had a very different ending had she not been blessed with a supportive community whose members lifted her up and helped her get her spirit moving. And now she is paying it forward by helping other survivors rise and thrive, too.

Sara isn't one to soft-pedal her struggle, and her story can be hard to read at times. But I don't want to suggest that *Any Body Can Heal* is a sad or depressing book. On the contrary, it's a powerful and uplifting read because it demonstrates that with courage, persistence, hard work and support, anything is possible—even facing down the most unspeakable trauma.

Marnie McBean, OLY
Three-time Olympic gold medalist
Officer of the Order of Canada
Canadian senator

Introduction

This is a book about how to find your way back from trauma. I've survived several traumatic events in my life. As a twenty-five-year-old student teaching in South Africa, I was robbed at knifepoint. At twenty-six, I was walking along a beach in Thailand when I was sucked underwater by a tsunami, then fled bleeding and in shock to the top of a hill, where I waited for days to be rescued. At thirty-two, while living in Trinidad, two masked gunmen burst through my bedroom door in the middle of the night and for hours took turns raping me.

At the time of the sexual assault, I was studying to become a psychotherapist. I had deliberately chosen to enroll in an online master's program that would allow me to pursue my studies while living abroad. After the sexual assault, when I eventually resumed my schooling, I found myself in the strange position of learning how to treat clients struggling with mental health issues that were preventing them from moving forward in their lives—while undergoing intensive therapy to put the pieces of my own back together.

After graduation, when I began building my practice, I decided I wanted to use my experience to help sexual assault survivors heal. Helping them heal, I believed, would help me heal as well because it would allow me to draw meaning from my pain. I knew I couldn't work with trauma survivors exclusively. Listening to their stories all day would be too difficult and enervating. I just knew I wanted to help them in some way.

When I first launched my practice, I took a part-time job working as a psychotherapist at a training college for dental hygienists to supplement my income. The students I worked with were under tremendous duress, struggling to cope with the demands of an intensely taxing and competitive program. In their appointments with me they reported panic attacks, sleep disturbances and such severe anxiety that some of them were harming themselves and having suicidal ideations.

To help myself understand what was prompting such extreme stress responses and help them grasp what was going on in their bodies to cause those reactions and learn how to manage them, I began researching the neuroscientific literature on trauma. During that process, I developed a deep theoretical understanding of the strategies the body employs to adapt to stress. Gradually, I came to see the students' symptoms—and ultimately my own—as the body's brilliant and beautiful mechanisms for adapting to stressful situations.

Then a remarkable thing happened. Gaining that awareness didn't just provide me with the knowledge and insight I needed to help the students understand and manage their trauma. It marked a turning point in my recovery. Even after all the therapy I'd had—including, among other interventions, a year and a half of intensive twice-weekly therapy sessions with a trauma-focused sensorimotor psychotherapist—that insight had a profound influence on my ability to heal. I came to see my body not as my enemy but as my friend—even a superhero. And I saw my symptoms not as a tyrannical force but as manifestations of my body's valiant efforts to protect me during a life-threatening situation. Both of these shifts in mindset changed everything for me. It was only after I was able to embrace my body as my saviour that I was finally able to make peace with what had happened to me and ultimately move forward.

Over the years, many people have encouraged me to write

a book about my experiences, but for a long time, I resisted. Talking about myself doesn't come easily to me. I'm a private person by nature. I also wrestled with the fact that while I've lived through terrible events, I'm hardly the first person to have suffered from trauma. Many survivors have horrific stories to tell. What was so unique about my experience that it warranted a book?

What's more, a great deal has been written about trauma over the last decade, much of it by experts far more knowledgeable on the subject than I am. What could I possibly have to add to that discussion? In the end, I decided that my personal experience coupled with what I've learned about the science of survival as well as working with sexual assault survivors gave me a unique perspective to offer. This book is a product of that learning.

I'm a big believer in resilience and finding the gold nuggets in life. I'm also a huge science-of-resilience nerd. For years, I found it triggering just to think about my trauma. It's a measure of how far I've come that I not only feel able to but also want to share my story—and in book form, no less.

The driving force behind my decision to write this book is my desire to help others suffering from trauma, especially sexual assault survivors. One of my most firmly held convictions is that with privilege comes responsibility. I'm in the extraordinarily privileged position of having a family that has provided me with unconditional love and support from day one and that was also in a position to help me financially and cover the cost of the intensive therapy I required. I'm also blessed to be surrounded by a loving circle of friends, many of whom stopped their lives to ensure that I had whatever I needed during my darkest hour. Many sexual assault survivors aren't so lucky. Above all, I wrote this book for them. My greatest hope is that by sharing my story, I will help them find their way, too.

I also wrote this book for therapists and other professionals who work with sexual assault survivors in the hope that they, too, will find something of value to take back with them to the therapy room. Perhaps my story of healing and resilience in the face of multiple traumas will serve as a resource to inform their work. Perhaps they will find it useful to recommend my story to their clients to help them feel validated and normalized as they navigate their journeys. Perhaps for some clients my story will serve as a testament that it is possible to make it through even their most despairing days. While no book can ever be a substitute for working with an experienced psychotherapist, I hope that for survivors who can't access or afford therapy, reading my story will at least help them feel less terrified and alone and provide them with the sense that they are connected to a community.

Although I primarily write in this book about my experience working with a sensorimotor psychotherapist, I also benefited from many other therapeutic approaches, including narrative therapy, polyvagal theory, acceptance and commitment therapy, mindfulness-based self-compassion therapy, dialectical behaviour therapy and others. At the back of the book, I have included resources and strategies drawn from various other approaches. They were helpful to me, and I hope they will also be helpful to readers.

Finally, I hope this book will offer some insight and consolation for the loved ones of sexual assault survivors. Trauma doesn't just savage the lives of those who survive it. It has a blast radius whose collateral damage extends far beyond the traumatized person. That said, an important piece of my healing was learning how to listen to my body and find my own path forward, even when my loved ones couldn't understand some of my choices or, as in some cases, those choices hurt or terrified them. But I needed to face down my trauma in my own way. I wrote this book in part because when I was in the trenches, I often wished the people I loved had a resource to help them understand a survivor's perspective and learn how to support a loved one who is struggling to manage a trauma response.

Some of my friends are still angry about what happened to me—angry with the men who hurt me, angry with me for not being angrier with the men. Some of the people who love me blame themselves for failing to protect me, however illogical that may be. What happened to me broke my parents' hearts, and nothing will ever mend them, no matter how far I have come. They are haunted by what happened. Rocked to their core. They will always feel that they failed to protect me, even though of course there is no way they could possibly have prevented the harm those men visited upon me or the suffering and sorrow I experienced in its wake. No parent can protect their child from the vicissitudes of life, however desperately they may wish to.

There were times while working on this book when I thought about how hard it was going to be for some of my family and friends to read parts of it. For a while, I thought that maybe there was some way I could put all the horrible stuff into one chapter and mark it with a trigger warning so they could skip over reading that chapter and I could protect them from having to endure more pain. But then I realized it doesn't work that way. Whether they choose to read this book in its entirety, in part, or at all is up to them, of course. But this is my story—my truth—and I have to tell it the way it happened. There's no way to sugarcoat what happened to me, no way to soften the blow. I can't protect my loved ones from knowing my truth any more than they could protect me from living it.

What will you find in these pages? I recount the three traumatic events I lived through and their impact, but my main focus is the sexual assault and my struggle to find my way back to the land of the living in its aftermath. I chose to focus mainly on the assault because it was by far the most devastating of the traumatic events, and coming back from it was by far my most difficult struggle. I have included neuroscientific information because learning about the neuroscience of trauma and its role in my survival and path to healing is so pivotal to the narrative. However, I have incorporated that information conversationally. This is not an academic or scientific tome. I also changed some people's names and identifying details out of respect for their privacy.

A note about my choice of language in the book. I use the word *rape* to describe what those men did to me, but I deliberately use it sparingly. I don't like that word. I think it's ugly, and even after all this time, I still find it triggering. Wherever possible, I prefer to use terms like *sexual assault* or *attack*. When I do use the word *rape*, I do so because in that instance it feels to me like the only word I can use that truly conveys the heinous nature of what those men took from me.

One last word: This has not been an easy book to write, and for some readers it will not be an easy book to read. While loss is an inescapable theme in a story like mine, at the end of the day this is not a story primarily about loss. It's a story about resilience and hope. It's also a story about pride—I'm proud of my body for protecting me. And I'm proud of myself for working so hard to resist succumbing to the darkness and stubbornly refusing to allow what happened to me that terrible night to define me or the rest of my life. My greatest wish is that you, too, will find resilience and hope in these pages.

PART ONE

BEFORE

Chapter One

FLIGHT

The water was doing strange things that morning. Nothing alarming. Just weird. Something about the current was off. The waves weren't rolling in towards shore the way they normally did. They were coming in at an odd angle. The water level was unusually low, too. The locals didn't seem concerned. *Full moon, spring tide,* they kept saying. Except it wasn't spring. It was Boxing Day, the day after Christmas, 2004.

I was vacationing with friends on Koh Phi Phi, a tiny, pristine island in the Andaman Sea off the southwest coast of Thailand, an hour or so ferry ride from Phuket. I was twenty-six and midway through my second year of teaching high school. Ordinarily, I wouldn't spend Christmas away from my family—I love Christmas so much that I keep my decorations up for months afterwards—but my friend Roxy, whom I've known since high school, was teaching at the Canadian International School in Singapore and I wanted to see her.

Travelling is in my DNA. I'd been globetrotting with my

family ever since my teen years and had developed a passion for seeing the world and meeting new people. When I travel, I just feel freer and more alive. So when Roxy moved, I knew I had to get over there. I met up with her and her then-boyfriend, Mark, in Singapore; we toured around for a bit, then headed to Koh Phi Phi.

The island of Koh Phi Phi is shaped like a peanut, with a narrow isthmus in the middle. The middle part—Tonsai Village—is where the town centre and markets are located and where all the action is. But we chose to stay in Long Beach, which is at the island's more peaceful southern end. Our hotel was perched high atop a steep hill overlooking the beach. We spent a couple of days there but planned to switch hotels that morning. We had to navigate about a hundred or so steps every time we wanted to go down to the beach or back up to our hotel. We wanted to find something closer to the beach.

It was around ten o'clock on Boxing Day morning. Roxy and I had checked out of the hotel, but Mark was taking his time checking out, so Roxy and I decided to go ahead and wait for him on the beach. After we made it down all the steps, I waded out into the water. That's when I first noticed the low water level and strange angle of the current. On previous days when I'd waded into the water, I had to wade out only a couple of feet before it came up to my knees. But that morning I could wade out quite far and it still hit me only around mid-shin.

At the time, I played soccer at a semiprofessional level and was doing exercises on that trip to repair my MCL, or medial collateral ligament, which I'd torn playing in the nationals that year. Ordinarily, I did my exercises on land. I couldn't do them in the water because I had to hinge my knee back and forth to perform that movement, and when the water came up to my knees, it created too much resistance. But that morning, when I lifted my foot to do my knee flexions and extensions, the water was so low it hit me around my lower shin and upper ankle, which was the perfect spot to press against its resistance. This was so striking that I shouted to Roxy back on the beach. "Hey, Roxy! Look, I can do my exercises!"

Mark soon joined us, and the three of us began walking along the beach towards the hotel we'd planned to check into that morning. It was a spectacular morning like every other we'd spent on the island, where the beauty of nature is so magnificent it feels almost otherworldly. The water was a pristine turquoise, and you could see the Thai longtail boats tied up at shore. The sand was that magical white colour, with soft, fine granules. Perfect palm trees lined the beach, and yellow, purple and red flora brightened the landscape. Still, despite the serenity of the setting, I must have had a sixth sense that something wasn't right, because as we were walking along, I turned to Roxy and said, "Wouldn't it be wild if this huge wave came and wiped out the whole island?"

Roxy was not amused. "Shut up," she said, shooting me side-eye. "Why would you say such a stupid thing?"

We kept on walking towards the hotel. A wave came up unusually far onto the beach—much farther than it reasonably should have. It was almost halfway to the hotels and restaurants at its outer edge, and in some places right up to them, then it receded so far and fast that people on the beach began to scream. Not panicked screams. More like startled, inquisitive ones. It was unsettling for the water to behave so aggressively, and people began to wonder what the hell was going on. The wave's behaviour unnerved us as well. As the wave came up onto the beach, it funnelled into a small canyon in the sand near where we were walking, deepening the canyon and pushing a girl into it. When she stood up, we saw that the wave had come in with such force that it had washed off her bikini top, and there was blood all over her back.

We decided to stop for a few minutes and wait for things to calm down. We were standing in front of an open-air restaurant at that point, about thirty feet back from the shoreline. We had just set our backpacks down and were standing with our backs to the water when a deafening noise, like the roar of a jet plane, came out of nowhere. The next thing I knew, a massive wall of water overtook me and I was underwater and the wave was spinning me around and turning me upside down and pummelling me from side to side. It was like being caught inside a giant washing machine. Every time the wave spun me around, all I could see was a chaotic blur of water and the sky flashing intermittently above me. My lungs began to burn. I didn't know how much longer I could hang on. I thought I was going to die. Then the water began dragging me in the opposite direction and slammed me violently against a hard surface. I couldn't tell what it was, but it felt like a pole, and I grabbed on to it and clung for dear life. Then, as suddenly as the wave had arrived and sucked me under, it receded, and I was standing on solid ground again. The whole thing had lasted maybe ten seconds.

Dazed, I looked around and saw that I was standing in the middle of the open-air restaurant—or at least what was left of it—about ten or fifteen feet ahead of where the three of us had set our backpacks down. The restaurant was miraculously still standing, but there was wreckage everywhere: upended tables and chairs, bent poles, an awning ripped and hanging. I looked down and saw that I was covered in blood and had nicks and cuts all over my body. I had a deep gash on my right knee and shin where the wave had slammed me into one of the metal poles holding up the restaurant's awning. Roxy and Mark were standing a few feet away. Roxy had a four-inch piece of wood sticking out of the back of her knee. Mark was cut up and limping back towards Roxy and me. Our backpacks were lying around in our general vicinity, where the wave had deposited them on its retreat. Mine was on the sand down by the water. A few dazed tourists were inside the restaurant with us. We stood there in stunned disbelief. No one spoke, but we were all thinking the same thing: *What the fuck was that?*

We had no idea what had just happened. We'd never heard of a tsunami. We just saw people on the beach running and screaming, heads bobbing in the water, arms frantically waving. It was immediately clear to us that some people had been swept out to sea. We had a brief discussion about staying put for a few minutes to get our bearings, but every instinct in my body was telling me that we had to get to higher ground. "No," I said. "We have to climb that hill." Roxy had pulled the piece of wood from the back of her knee, and blood was starting to seep from the wound. We wrestled into our backpacks and started running towards the hill. But we were injured, our waterlogged backpacks felt like cement blocks, and the hill was thick with vegetation. The only way we could make it up was by bear crawling and grabbing rocks and tree roots to pull ourselves up while scrub and vegetation rained down upon us.

It took us about ten minutes to make it to the top, which was covered in dense jungle. We found a clearing and dropped our backpacks. Mark immediately started going up and down the hill to help bring up more of the wounded, while Roxy and I began madly pulling shirts out of our backpacks and ripping them apart to make tourniquets to staunch our bleeding.

A few other survivors had made it to the top ahead of us. Most were bleeding and in shock. Some were crying hysterically or emitting terrified, ear-piercing screams. Some were Thai locals. They kept saying another wave was coming. We had no idea if that was true. If they were right, we didn't know if we were high enough to be out of harm's way or if we'd be swept away. We couldn't see the beach from our vantage point. There were no sight lines. Too much dense vegetation was in the way. We found out the Thai locals were right when we heard a sudden round of terrified screams coming from below.

We stayed at the top of the hill for the rest of the day. We stayed because we didn't know what else to do. More and more of the injured came up the hill all day. When the wave hit, flying chunks of galvanized steel from the roofs of collapsing beach huts had left such deep gouges on some of the survivors' bodies, they looked as if they'd been sliced with a butcher's knife. In other cases, the wave had tossed them around so violently that they had broken noses.

I was desperate to get word to my parents. They were in New York and wouldn't have heard the news yet because of the time difference. But none of our phones were working. They were too waterlogged. That afternoon I managed to borrow a phone from a Danish woman and leave them a voicemail. I told them something horrible had happened, that I was injured and didn't know if I was going to make it out. I told them that whatever happened, I loved them very much.

By nightfall, around twenty of us were lying at the top of the hill, hurt, hungry and still in shock. Rumours continued to swirl. Some people said a third wave was coming, but it was all hearsay. Nobody knew for sure. We had no idea whom to believe or what to do. Say a third wave did come—where would we run? And how? Even if we could run with our injuries, could we even make it down the hill? And then what? Where would we go? But spending the night in the jungle didn't seem like a viable alternative, either. People kept saying the jungle was full of poisonous snakes. I am petrified of snakes.

Eventually, we decided to return to the hotel we'd checked out of that morning. It was so high up on the cliff that we knew it would still be intact. We hoisted our backpacks again and started making our way over. By the time we arrived, the hotel was teeming with so many survivors that it looked like a mini refugee camp. The staff packed as many of us into rooms as they could. The rest of us slept outside. We got lucky. We slept on the floor of the room of a couple whom Roxy and Mark had befriended when we were guests at the hotel and who hadn't gone down to the beach that morning. It was after we got to the hotel that we started to hear the truly horrific stories. Some people who'd travelled to the island as a group of four were down to three or two. Some had narrowly escaped drowning when their hotel rooms filled with water. One woman had had her child ripped out of her hands.

We spent the second day waiting around, desperately hoping to be rescued. We had no idea how long we'd be at the top of that hill. We managed to eat a meal of chicken and rice in the hotel restaurant but didn't know how soon the hotel would run out of food. By then, news reports had started to trickle in. We watched footage of the devastation on the TV in the hotel restaurant. We saw the wreckage in other parts of the island and Thailand, as well as in Sri Lanka and Indonesia, but we didn't absorb the enormity of the event. Not yet. It was still too hard to fathom. We were still too much in the middle of it. Still too in shock.

Later that day an army boat came in with a helicopter on deck, and soldiers began removing the dead bodies from the island along with anyone so severely injured that they weren't going to survive unless they got to a hospital. At some point that day I borrowed a cell phone and texted my dad. I told him we'd made it to the hotel and were going to be okay. He texted me back immediately and instructed me to get to Bangkok airport and he'd meet us there.

On our third day waiting to be rescued, the army came and took the rest of us down from the hill. When we learned it was our turn to leave, we strapped on our backpacks and joined the line snaking its way down the stairs to the beach. Sun burnished, in tattered clothing, filthy, sweating, we looked like *Survivor* contestants emerging from the jungle. Except this was no reality show. It was real life. I still had on the same sports bra and basketball shorts I had been wearing when the tsunami hit. The only difference was that now I was barefoot. The wave had washed away my flip-flops.

We headed down the beach towards the Zodiac that was

waiting to carry us to the army boat anchored offshore. From there we had a two-hour ferry ride to Krabi, where we'd try to wrangle a flight to Bangkok airport. As we walked along, my eyes landed on a surreal sight amid all the devastation: my flip-flops were lying side by side, undisturbed on the sand in the middle of the beach. Someone had clearly placed them there for their owner to reclaim. I stared at them for a moment, trying to process what I was seeing. Then I continued walking in their direction, slid my feet inside, and kept on walking towards the Zodiac—and home.

❋❋❋

The tsunami wasn't the first traumatic event of my life, nor would it be the last or even the most devastating. I've had so much experience dealing with trauma that I've spent most of my adult life trying to navigate it. If I've learned anything about the subject—and I've learned a lot—it's that trauma can be a tough taskmaster. And a formidable opponent. Every time I thought I'd outsmarted it, it found a way to outmanoeuvre me. Trauma can be wily that way. Sometimes living with trauma is like living with an uninvited guest who refuses to leave. But as difficult and exhausting as trauma can be, it's possible to show it the door. Of that I'm living proof.

Learning how to navigate trauma has taught me a lot about resilience. I would have much preferred to have learned those lessons in other ways. But that's not what life had in store for me. Still, despite all the suffering I've had to endure, I consider myself one of the lucky ones. There are many reasons for that, but one of the biggest is this: If you want to put trauma behind you or learn to live with it and move on with your life, it helps to have a loving support system around you. And in that respect I have been blessed.

Chapter Two

CHARMED LIFE

If you don't count the three terrifying events I've lived through, I've led a pretty charmed life. I was born in Vancouver, British Columbia, in 1978, almost at the tail end of Generation X, that statistically insignificant, so-called forgotten generation sandwiched between two noisier and more attention-grabbing ones: baby boomers and millennials. I'm fine with that timing since attention seeking is not my thing.

We moved around a lot during my early childhood. My dad was a geologist whose work took him into the bush for months at a time to conduct field studies at mining sites. When I was eight months old, we moved to La Ronge, a former fur-trading post on the western shore of Lac la Ronge in northern Saskatchewan. The town sits in the middle of the boreal forest and is surrounded by First Nations reserves. My mom said it was so cold there that the curtains in our rental house froze. La Ronge, which means "the chewed," is said to have been named by early French fur traders, presumably because

a significant number of its profuse beaver population chewed
and toppled shoreline trees to build their dams.

Shortly after we arrived, my dad had to head into the inte-
rior for a couple of months to work on a site. Before my parents
moved to BC, my mom had taught primary school and English
as a second language in Montreal. When I was a year old, she
took a teaching job on a Cree reserve and put me in daycare,
which was housed in a trailer on the reserve. One of my first
words was *nikâwiy*, which is Cree for "mother." When I was
three we moved again, this time to Thunder Bay, in Northern
Ontario, where my brother, Travis, was born. A couple of years
later we returned to Vancouver, where my parents put down
roots and I started kindergarten. But those peripatetic formative years helped foster my wanderlust.

If you're lucky enough to have had a happy childhood, as I
did, you tend to view yours through rose-coloured glasses. But
looking back I can honestly say that mine was nearly picture
perfect. We lived in Kitsilano, fourteen blocks from the beach
and fifteen minutes from downtown, and we shared our mod-
est two-storey house on West Fourteenth Avenue with a ro-
tating menagerie of dogs, cats, turtles, hamsters, guinea pigs,
lizards and neighbourhood kids. Our street was swarming
with kids. On any given day, so many drifted in and out of our
house that we had to buy Freezies in bulk in case a small hungry army of them needed a sugar rush. Nobody locked their
doors, which gave us kids license to roam freely through our
neighbours' backyards and in and out of their houses whenever we played hide-and-seek or capture the flag. Our family
had hockey nets set up in our basement, so a couple of kids
were always hanging out downstairs, and my friends and I
played street hockey for hours on end in the big alleyways behind our houses.

I was a happy-go-lucky kid, confident and independent-
minded (some might say stubborn), who excelled at sports and

academics. My mom taught French at our local elementary school (she taught my brother and me for a while), worked at the local daycare attached to the school and held down the fort at home. Meanwhile, my dad travelled for months at a time. I missed him when he was gone, but he always came home for important days such as birthdays, Thanksgiving, Christmas, Easter and my big sporting events.

I was a sports kid from the get-go. Stereotypically girl-ish pursuits didn't interest me. Indoors, I played with Hot Wheels, G.I. Joes and Micro Machines. But I was rarely in-doors. Mostly I was outdoors—climbing, running races, kick-ing a soccer ball around and playing street hockey with the boys. When I played with the boys, I didn't just hold my own. Often I beat them. I was strong, athletically built, agile and fast, and I thrived on the action and adrenaline. I didn't feel the need to show off when I scored or saved the game with a last-minute slide tackle on an opponent. I was happy to slip under the radar. Mostly I just loved the way I felt playing sports: strong, present and free.

Since I mostly hung out with boys, most of my friends were boys. But I didn't just play sports with them. I looked and dressed like them, too. One of my BFFs growing up was Josh Jackson, who later played Pacey on *Dawson's Creek*. We had identical mullets with rattails down the back. We looked like twins.

During my elementary and middle school years, I played baseball, basketball, soccer, volleyball, track and field, and any other sport for which I could try out and compete, but soc-cer was always my favourite game and the one I excelled at most. My mom says my talent for the sport presented itself early. I was a ferocious kicker in the womb. Besides my brother, who's also athletic, no one else in my family has any athletic gifts whatsoever, so we can't figure out where the talent comes from. My mom likes to claim she's good at badminton, but her assertion invariably elicits eye rolls and merciless teasing from the rest of us.

When I was thirteen, my life turned upside down. My dad was offered an executive position at a Canadian mining company with operating sites around the globe. The company was headquartered in Toronto, so we had to move. I was devastated when I learned this news. I had zero agency in the decision, and Vancouver was the epicentre of my universe. It was where I'd grown up, where all my friends were. Having everything I cherished unceremoniously snatched away from me felt utterly destabilizing. How could I possibly replicate that experience in another city? Plus I'd just entered my first year of high school, which began in grade eight in BC but a year later in Ontario, so I'd have to start high school all over again. How could my parents persecute me in this way? To make matters worse, I'd just begun to find my way on my sports teams. I was certain that having to move was the most traumatic thing anyone could be forced to endure, and I hated my dad for being the cause of my misery. I vowed I would never talk to him again. And for months, I didn't.

That summer we moved to a northern Toronto suburb. In the fall, I started grade nine at Earl Haig Secondary School. A few days in, the athletic department held tryouts for the girls' basketball team. Since I was the newbie, the coach asked two grade-ten students to partner with me for tryouts. One of the girls was Roxy. The other, Eva. All three of us wound up making the team. I soon learned I might have overreacted a bit to having to move. Thanks to Roxy and Eva, navigating the transition to my new school was relatively painless. They took me under their wings, introduced me around and made sure I had someone to sit with in the cafeteria. Two months later, volleyball season rolled around, and a few months after that, soccer and baseball season. The three of us made those teams, too.

Pretty soon they were my besties. To this day, they remain two of my closest friends.

I wound up loving high school. As always, sports were at the centre of my life, and through sports, I made a whole batch of new friends. Soccer, basketball and volleyball were my top three games, but I was blessed to be able to pick up pretty much any sport I tried. Outside school, I played club basketball and soccer. My schedule was wild. I played one sport or another three times a day. But I loved sports so much that playing round the clock never felt like an imposition.

On weekdays I was at school before seven for morning practice. I usually had a game or practice after school, came home, ate dinner, and most weeknights had a club basketball or soccer game. My club teams travelled around Ontario for tournaments a lot. So did my school teams, but less so. The tournaments were the best, especially for basketball. We stayed in hotel rooms and competed with friends. It was ridiculously fun. Besides the camaraderie and thrill of competing, I also loved the hard work we put in together and the showing up for one another, although I don't think I fully appreciated the value of that experience at the time. I never did drugs in high school—never even experimented—probably because I got such a rush from playing sports that it was the only high I needed.

Staying motivated in sports was never a problem. Academics, not so much. I wasn't great at sitting. Somehow, though, I managed to get good grades. Math and science were my strong subjects. English—the bane of my existence. I don't think I ever actually read a Shakespeare play. (Sorry, Mr. Shakira.) In those pre-internet, pre-ChatGPT days, I read Coles Notes plot summaries the night before a test or exam and extrapolated whatever I needed to get by. As for my romantic life, I dated and had boyfriends during high school, but only if they accepted my sacrosanct rule: sports came first.

In grade nine, on tryout day for a soccer club I hoped to join in Scarborough, I walked into a gym teeming with kids, didn't know a soul, and saw this gangly, long-limbed, brown-skinned girl with a tiny peanut-shaped head and cool vibe about her sitting on the floor with her back against the gym wall. She had on a gigantic pair of headphones and was rocking her head to the beat. Drawn to her, I headed over, and she offered me a seat beside her on the floor. I asked what she was listening to. "Reggae," she said. "Do you want to listen?" she asked, handing me her headphones. "Sure," I said, then put them on and started bopping my head to the music. "I'm Odia," she said. And that was the beginning of another beautiful lifelong relationship.

Odia and I played soccer together in that Scarborough club throughout high school, competing at the provincial and national level. In grade twelve, the University of Toledo scouted us independently for athletic scholarships. We toured the campus together and both signed on, although she committed long before I did.

Anyone who knows me knows that I'm allergic to commitment—in life and love. I much prefer to keep my options open as long as I possibly can, lest by choosing one door I foreclose on another that might offer me rosier possibilities. As soon as I make a decision, I invariably start worrying that I've made the wrong one and begin to feel trapped. I fear if I make the wrong choice that I'll limit my options, and once I commit, there's no going back. (My therapist has much to say on this theme.)

Odia and I headed to Toledo in the fall of 1997. For the next four years, we roomed together and threw ourselves wholeheartedly into the American college experience. When you go to an American sports college, sports are all you do, so I was in my happy place, and since Ohio is only a short hop from

Toronto, I could travel back and forth to see my friends and family, and my parents could come down regularly to watch me play.

No matter the sport, I'm always a defensive player. Remember earlier when I mentioned I've never been one to crave the spotlight? That applies to sports, too. The position you play isn't just a reflection of your athletic talents. It can also say a lot about your personality. As much as I love to compete, I don't like to be in the limelight. In volleyball, I'm a setter. My job isn't to spike the ball. It's to set it up for my teammates so they can. In ball hockey, rather than raising my stick when I score, I'm much more comfortable turning around and acknowledging the player who set me up. In soccer, when I gain possession of the ball, I much prefer to pass it to another player and let them score.

Defenders may not be as technically adept as strikers at handling the ball, but they're harder hitters. And while strikers often flail around and are easier to bump off the ball, defenders are grittier. They're also steadier and hold down the game. There's a saying in sports that offense wins games, but defense wins championships. That's because the defender is the player who has to be ready at all times, keep at it and never waver. The defender is the anchor and the foundation of the team. The rock, not the rock star.

After four exhilarating, exhausting years at Toledo, I graduated with a bachelor's in exercise science. I thought about pursuing a career in the fitness industry, so after college, I took a year off from school to work in a gym as a personal trainer. But the company I worked for was extremely sales driven, and I decided that wasn't the life for me. Instead, I resolved to become a gym teacher. I'd coached a lot of kids at sports and had enjoyed mentoring them, so I figured becoming a high school gym teacher would be a good fit. I also loved travelling and discovering other cultures. Having a teaching degree under my belt would give me the flexibility to teach abroad. But if I'm being totally honest, I also opted to go to teacher's college because teaching was the only career I'd considered where I would have to complete just one year of schooling before I could start working. Less sitting! I entered teachers college in the fall of 2002 and began working towards earning a secondary school teaching degree in science and physical education. I was twenty-four years old and thirsty for the knowledge and practical classroom experience that I'd need to launch my career.

Chapter Three

AFTERSHOCKS

The main thing about trauma that messes with your head—the thing that trumps all the other things—is the way it guts your sense of safety. After you live through a traumatic event, what you can't replace, certainly not easily and maybe not ever, is your belief that the world is a fundamentally safe place. Trauma steals that from you and replaces it with the knowledge that the world is menacing, a place where you always have to be on guard.

For the first few months after I returned from Thailand, I was constantly glancing over my shoulder, scanning the room for potential threats in the manner of a spy or Secret Service agent. If I was standing in a line, I did a quick threat evaluation of the person standing behind me. If I entered a room, the first thing I did was check the exits. If anything went down, I would know where to run. If I went to a restaurant, I always found a spot where I could position myself with my back to the wall. I didn't want any surprises from behind. I could never truly relax or be in the moment in such a hyperaware state. But if I secured my surroundings, I could let down my guard to some degree.

After I made it home, I took a few weeks off before I returned to teaching. Afterwards, I taught my classes. I played sports. I functioned. But for the better part of a year, my heart wasn't in anything I did. I was in a perpetually sullen mood, although for the most part I tried to hide it, which was exhausting. I lost interest in eating. I lost interest in seeing my friends, which for me was a huge red flag because before then I could barely go five minutes without seeing my friends. I had to fill every single moment of every single day with them.

Mostly what I wanted to do, especially in the first few months after I returned home, was watch footage of the tsunami. I watched it obsessively for hours. Although I'd seen some footage on the television in the hotel restaurant when we were waiting to be rescued, it wasn't until returning home that I truly understood the magnitude of the seismic event I'd lived through. Once I was home, it hit me with full force. That's when I learned what a tsunami was: how it's set off by an earthquake that sends out shock waves that don't crest, and how the one that hit the island was thirty metres high. That's when I watched footage of it swallowing the middle of the island from both sides, decimating it and killing thousands.

Although I didn't understand this at the time, I now know that obsessively watching the footage was a coping mechanism. I was looking for some way to make sense of what I'd been through and integrate its meaning about the fragility of life into my understanding of the world, even though horror of that magnitude is incomprehensible. To come to terms with it, I had to desensitize myself and somehow make it feel less overwhelming. Obsessively watching the footage was one way for me to do that. But looking back, I think I also watched it repetitively to distract myself from thinking dark thoughts.

I was consumed with dark thoughts. I kept seeing images I couldn't unsee. Horrific images. Like the image of the little boy I watched being carried out to sea that day. I kept seeing the terror in his eyes as he was swept away. I was haunted by that image. It was seared into my memory. I kept thinking about all the people whose lives were snuffed out in an instant. I was haunted by thoughts of drowning. When I was in the wave, I came way too close to knowing what it would feel like to drown. I knew that clawing your way to suffocation would be a horrifying way to die.

I had thoughts like that all the time. Then I had to teach my classes and go about the routines of my daily life. But all I wanted to do was go home and watch the footage. Teaching my classes and going about the routines of daily life felt utterly dislocating. Watching the footage was the only thing that felt real to me at the time. Watching it allowed me to reconnect with others who'd been through what I had and made me feel less alone. I felt deeply, painfully alone because nobody around me understood what I was going through.

I was tortured with guilt. I'd read estimates that almost 4,000 people had perished on the island that day—almost 250,000 if you counted the people who died in all the other countries the tsunami hit. But I didn't perish, did I? Inexplicably, I survived. Then I fled to the top of the hill and made it to the hotel where the Thai people fed me and brought me Popsicles to stay hydrated. Then I was plucked out of the devastation and got to return home and carry on with my life surrounded by people overjoyed to have me back. Meanwhile thousands upon thousands suffered unfathomable loss and were left to deal with the devastation and sorrow.

I struggled mightily to make sense of the incomprehensibility of it all. I kept thinking about how Roxy, Mark and I had gone to dinner in town the night before the tsunami hit. What if we'd decided to go to town the next morning? We'd almost certainly have died. Why were we spared? That question tormented me. I must have turned it over in my mind a thousand times. There was no answer, at least not one that satisfied me. The only logical conclusion I could come to was that the universe was a randomly cruel place.

For many months afterwards, family and friends kept trying to comfort me, but the more they attempted to console me, the more I waved them away. Even under normal circumstances, I'm inclined to brush off others' attempts to fuss over me. I don't accept help easily. If I'm injured playing sports, I tend to downplay my pain. After the tsunami, that inclination was off the charts. At the time, I was living with friends. They kept cooking meals for me and leaving them outside my bedroom door. My response wasn't to thank them for their kindness. It was to scold them for taking care of me. *I don't deserve this. Why aren't you worrying about the people who lost everything? They need it much more than I do.*

I now know I was suffering from survivor's guilt. Refusing their help and telling myself I didn't deserve it was my self-inflicted penance for surviving, a way of expiating my guilt for living when so many others had died. For months afterwards, I repeated what I thought I believed to be true: *Don't worry about me. I'm fine.* Even though it was abundantly clear to everyone except me that I was not fine.

My mom begged me to see someone, but I refused to go to a therapist. I'd never been one to talk about my feelings. I'm much more inclined to suck them up. I'm a lot like my dad in that way. As a kid, when I fell and started to cry, my mom picked me up, cuddled me and wiped away my tears. My dad told me to get up and stop crying. Stoicism always served me well as an athlete. I learned to be tough on the field, push through my injuries and keep going. But trying to be stoic in the face of trauma, I've learned, is not a good plan. When you've been through a horrific event, sucking up your feelings and pretending everything's okay isn't a sign of strength. It's a sign of denial. Eventually, my mom wore me down, and I agreed to see our family doctor. I went to her office once a week for a few weeks, sitting there and talking while she listened.

I was equally heedless about my physical health. When we made it to the Bangkok airport and checked in with the Red Cross, an aid worker told us to have our injuries checked out at the hospital emergency room after we arrived home. We'd done our best to clean our wounds when we were at the top of that hill, but by the time I returned home, the huge gash on my leg from the wave slamming me into the pole had started to emit yellow pus. My mom kept urging me to have the wound looked at, but I was in no rush to go to the hospital. Finally, I relented.

When I went to emergency and told the person at the front desk that I'd been in the tsunami, I quickly regretted my decision. She immediately began yelling, "We have a survivor here! We have a survivor here!" and a flock of hospital staff fluttered to my side. I found the attention unbearable and waved them away. *I'm fine. I didn't die. Take care of all the people in worse shape than me.* They called in a social worker to talk to me, but I waved her off, too. It didn't seem to occur to me that I'd survived an earthquake and been airlifted out of a disaster zone and that my psyche might be working overtime trying to process what I'd been through—that I, too, might need some help.

Chapter Four

FIGHT

To graduate teachers college, I had to complete three practice teaching assignments in addition to my coursework. I completed the first two at local high schools, but I was allowed to do the third anywhere in the world as long as the school met certain criteria. I decided to look abroad and chose to do my last one in South Africa. Aside from wanting to see the country, I chose South Africa because I had a cousin who lived in Durban and I knew I could stay with her. Through a contact of hers, I was able to secure a two-month internship teaching at a primary school. (Although I was training to become a secondary school teacher, students could complete a practicum anywhere that helped them grow as teachers.) In May, I boarded a flight to Durban.

The school was located in the townships, one of the poor residential areas designated for nonwhites during apartheid. The legacy of apartheid persists in South Africa. Its citizens still see themselves and one another in racial terms; the races

live in different areas and don't intermingle much. White peo-
ple are at the top of the pecking order, followed by Indians,
Black people, and "Coloureds," a self-referring term South
Africans use to describe being mixed race. My cousin lived in
Musgrave, a relatively upscale majority-white neighbourhood.
Each morning I walked about ten minutes from her flat to a
main thoroughfare, where one of the teachers picked me up
and I carpooled to school with a few other teachers.

My students were between six and eleven years old. Most
were Zulu, but I also taught a few Indian kids. They sat at long
horizontal desks, about sixty or seventy to a classroom, and
were generally orderly and well behaved. But they were just
kids, after all, and if one of them giggled or spoke out of turn,
it was not uncommon for me to see a teacher smash a ruler
down hard on their head or hand.

Most of them had probably never seen a white person
before, so I was an object of intense fascination. For the first
few days, they gazed at me with great curiosity, especially fascinated by my long curly blonde hair. One little girl finally
mustered the courage to come up to me and, with a nervous
giggle, tentatively reach out and touch my hair. After she made
the first move, the floodgates opened, and all the other girls
crowded around me, vying for the chance to touch it. Having
long hair was unfathomable to them. Theirs was almost completely shorn because nobody had the time or inclination to
care for it.

The kids were gorgeous in that radiant way that children
have, but their lives were rampant with trauma. They lived in
shantytowns, often in one-room shacks made of cardboard
boxes, often without proper sanitation, water or electricity.
They came to school in the same filthy clothes every day. Most
had scabies or tuberculosis sores on their faces, and many
were infected with HIV/AIDS. The virus was raging in their
communities. Children were contracting it at staggering rates,

either because they'd been born to an HIV-positive mother or had been raped by an infected man who believed the Zulu myth that you can cleanse your blood of the disease by having sex with a virgin child. Witnessing their suffering was difficult, but for me, seeing their smiles, smiling in return, and offering them whatever love and protection I could while I was their teacher outweighed the challenges that I had to deal with as I worked in that environment.

A few weeks into my internship, on a beautiful morning in late May, the school held a sports day in a huge gated field behind the building. About 150 kids were out in the field that morning, running races and kicking balls around under their teachers' supervision. My students were set to run a relay race and were huddled around me while I was crouched down in front of them in my T-shirt, basketball shorts and beaded African sandals, doing my best to explain to them how a relay works. Given the language barrier, I demonstrated how they had to grab the baton and run as fast as they could towards their classmate on the other side, then pass it to them and run back as fast as they could.

As I gesticulated with the baton, suddenly, and in unison, their eyes opened wide, and they froze in terror. Then I heard a male voice behind me say, "Give me your watch." Then all I heard was the sound of chaos and people running and screaming and the caterwauling wails of the teacher they had grabbed.

I couldn't see the man behind me. I could just feel him trying to pull me backwards and grab the watch off my right wrist. He was after my Nike bracelet watch. If I'd been thinking at that moment, I'd have slipped it off my wrist and handed it to him. I would have done that even if it was a family heirloom, which it wasn't. It cost fifty dollars and had no sentimental value to me whatsoever. But I wasn't thinking. I was acting on pure instinct.

I was jacked up on adrenaline. My heart was racing, and my breath was coming faster and faster. I tried to buck my attacker off my back. Each time I tried, he reached to grab my watch. We went a few rounds like this. Me trying to buck him off. Him trying to grab my watch. Every time we went another round, it ended in a draw. "You're so strong, so strong," I heard him say.

The next thing I knew, I felt an object pressing into my back. I felt pressure but not pain. My assailant pressed harder. That time, whatever he was holding broke my skin, and I flinched. In that instant, he snatched the watch from my wrist. Then I heard gunfire and saw security guards running out of the school, guns blazing.

I hit the deck. Most of the kids had fled when the ruckus started, but a few were still gaping and frozen in place. As I dived for cover, I pulled them down with me. I lay there, heart pounding, face pressed into the ground for a few moments. The gunfire stopped. Then silence, except for the horrific wails of the teacher. Slowly, people began lifting their heads to see if the intruders were gone. When it was clear they had fled, I stood up and began brushing myself off. When I was on my feet, my students rushed to my side and began hugging me ferociously, pointing to my muscles and shouting *"Amandla! Amandla!"* the Zulu word for "strength."

After we took the kids back up to their classrooms, I went to the staff room. I was shaky, my teeth were chattering, and I was holding back tears. The Indian teacher whose screams I'd heard during the melee had a broken arm. One of the robbers had broken it trying to yank off her gold bangle. Someone had called an ambulance for her. Until it arrived, a couple of staff members were trying to create a makeshift splint out of a few rulers. I learned that three robbers had broken into the field through an opening in the surrounding fence. The one who'd attacked me had dug a cutlass into my back. Eventually, the police arrived and asked me some questions. After the ambulance took the Indian teacher away, I returned to my classroom. I was still trembling and on the verge of tears but somehow managed to make it through the rest of the teaching day.

I knew my cousin wouldn't be home from work when my carpool dropped me off. As was my custom after school, I went to a nearby internet café and emailed a few friends. I didn't mention what had happened. I was too shaken and didn't feel like getting into the whole story in an email. It was only later, when I was back at my cousin's flat and called home and heard my mom's voice, that I began to sob and sob.

I returned to teaching classes the next day. I could have cut my practice-teaching stint short, but I wanted to finish my last few weeks. Despite the events of the previous day, I wasn't ready to leave yet. Something about being in that school with those kids brought me joy, and I didn't want that joy stolen from me. For the balance of my time there, I remained on edge and easily startled, but by the time I flew home, the initial shock of the trauma had worn off, and I didn't spend months moping around afterwards. I dived right back into playing sports and partying with my friends.

Being back on Canadian soil seemed to quiet the effects of the knife assault. From time to time, if my friends and I were waiting in line to enter a venue and there were strangers standing behind us, or if someone screamed or jolted me, I still felt on edge and started looking for exits. But for the most part, life just seemed to go on.

After I was robbed, my mind went to different places than it would after the tsunami. After Thailand, I never feared getting caught in another tsunami, since the odds of that happening were infinitesimal. After the robbery, however, I was less sure that I would never live through an experience like it again. The teachers told me the school had never had an incident like that in its forty-year history. My cousin had lived in Durban for five years at that point and hadn't experienced anything similar, either. And yet I'd been there only a couple of months, and it had happened to me. I began to think maybe there was something about *me* that caused this life-threatening event to happen. Maybe *I* did something to bring it them upon myself. For a while, that thought burrowed into my consciousness, and I couldn't get it out.

***

I flew home from Durban at the end of June and right away had to get busy looking for a teaching job for the fall. Unfortunately, I'd graduated into a tough job market, and nobody was hiring. September rolled around, then October. Nada. As Thanksgiving approached, I got lucky. I landed a job at Newtonbrook Secondary School, in North York, teaching math and science to grades nine and ten. It was only a one-year contract, and I wouldn't get to teach physical education, but it was a foot in the door. After the year was up, I was "surplussed" to Western Technical-Commercial School downtown for a year and assigned to teach in a class with students with individualized education programs.

That was the year I tore my knee ligament and had to hobble around on crutches for most of it as well as go to rehab after school. It was also the year I fled a tsunami, so all in all not the best year.

But then I heard about a position that had opened up at Emery Collegiate, a high school in the city's northwest quadrant. Emery was known for having a great physical education department and a basketball coach who was held in high esteem. On the flip side, it was a tough school. There were drugs. There were gangs. There was family violence. If I got the gig, I'd be teaching kids contending with serious issues who came from wildly different backgrounds than my own. But the prospect of teaching in tougher classrooms appealed to me. Plus, I'd finally get to teach phys ed and coach sports. When I learned I got the job, I was ecstatic.

I taught at Emery for four years. I loved my time teaching there. My students were labelled "behavioural" or "at-risk" by the school board, but I've never been fond of such labels, and it was both my job and my joy to ignore those words and find ways to connect with them as people and help them learn. During the last two years I taught at Emery, I had the opportunity to participate in a pilot program to help kids who'd dropped out of school because they lacked the credits to graduate. If a student had a failing grade in math, say, I helped them gain the basic math skills they needed to recover their credits.

There were only eight kids in a class in that program, so I had the chance to work one-on-one and develop a rapport with the students. In addition to helping them learn, I talked to them about what was going on in their lives—what was happening at home, how they were coping with the pressures of gang life and the various other difficulties they faced. Our worlds may have been galaxies apart, but I had some of the most real conversations with the kids in that program that I'd ever had with anyone in my life.

As much as I loved teaching at Emery, I decided to take a six-month leave of absence during the latter half of my second year. I was twenty-nine by then and felt the need to be a free bird for a while. I decided to spend six months travelling through Africa and Southeast Asia. I sublet my apartment, then joined up with one of my soccer teammates who also wanted to travel, and together we mapped a route: Hong Kong, the Philippines, Vietnam, Cambodia, Malaysia, Singapore, Ethiopia, Swaziland (now Eswatini), Tanzania and South Africa. I called it my *Eat Pray Love* trip.

During my travels, I had moments when some residual

effects of the knife assault lingered in my system. They manifested as an anxious feeling when I shared a taxi with a stranger, a rush of fear when I walked down a dark foreign street, or accelerated breathing if someone nudged me from behind in a busy market. However, the thrill and sense of freedom I felt as a traveller quickly silenced those feelings.

In the fall of 2007, after my travels, I returned to Emery renewed and ready to throw myself back into teaching. Life was great. I loved my students. I was seeing my friends. I was playing sports a thousand times a week. But it wasn't long before I started to get itchy again.

I had long had a hankering to teach abroad. In addition to our family trips to Mexico, Costa Rica and Tanzania in my teen years, during university I also had the opportunity to play soccer in Iceland one summer. Those experiences whet my appetite to explore other locales and cultures, and during my leave of absence, I was seriously bitten by the travel bug. So when a Trinidadian friend on a men's soccer team I played on approached me at a game one night and told me he was applying to teach at the Maple Leaf International School in Trinidad—and that there was an opening to teach phys ed that he thought would be perfect for me—I said to myself: *This is exactly what I need to do for a couple of years.*

Trinidad was an easy choice for me. I was already deeply familiar with the country and culture. Many of my closest friends were from Trinidad, as were most of the guys on my men's soccer team. I spent a major part of my twenties going with my friends to Toronto's annual Caribbean Carnival and on boat cruises in Toronto harbour, where we would dance the night away to reggae and soca music. Many of my Trinidadian friends had relatives and friends who lived on the island. I was sure I'd have an insta-community to watch over me. I also knew that a lot of my friends would come down and visit me during the year.

Ever since high school, I have had so many West Indian friends in my immediate circle that for as long as I can remember, I'm often the only white Canadian person wherever I go. I know their parents, their aunties and uncles. I've been a frequent guest in their homes. I've attended their Christmas dinners and Easter celebrations. I feel embraced by their warm, welcoming community and utterly at home in their vibrant culture.

I wasn't naïve about the country's problems. So many of the Trinidadians I'd met in Canada had come north to escape the poverty and violence back home. I knew the island had rough neighbourhoods. But I knew which parts to avoid. And the school would put me up in safe accommodations. I'd also travelled enough by then to know how to take care of myself. The only downside I could see was the pay, which wasn't great. I'd earn enough to live on, but I wouldn't be able to bank much. In every other respect, the job sounded perfect. So when my friend told me he'd been hired and would be teaching at the school in the fall, applying seemed like a no-brainer. I was offered a position teaching phys ed and math for a year. I gave up my apartment, stored my belongings and sold my car, and in August, my eyes wide with excitement, my stomach churning with nervous anticipation about what the future had in store for me, I eagerly set off on the next big adventure and phase of my life.

Chapter Five

PEAK JOY

The Maple Leaf International School, which is located just outside Port of Spain, caters to Trinidadian kids whose parents see them going on to university in Canada, the UK or the US. Except for a few local Trini teachers, all the instructors are certified to teach in Ontario schools, and the students study an Ontario curriculum. After graduation, many go on to pursue higher education abroad, and after they complete their studies, many return home to live and work.

I shared a house that year with Holly and Xavier, two other Canadians who'd also come down to teach. The house was within walking distance of the school. Mornings, Holly and I walked to school, always stopping along the way at one of the roadside stands to pick up doubles, which are sandwich patties made of fried dough filled with curried chickpeas. Holly is almost six feet tall, and we're both athletically built. As we passed by, the locals often called out to us, "Strong girls. Strong girls."

It was an incredible year—easily one of the best of my life. My days were filled with teaching, coaching soccer (or football, as Trinidadians call it) and going for runs with friends around the Savannah, a large park in Port of Spain. As I anticipated, I quickly found a crew to hang out with. Fridays after school, some of my colleagues and I headed down to a local rum shop called the Daybreak Café to grab a few beers, listen to music and unwind. On my way home I often stopped at Don's Roti Shop to pick up my regular dinner order of curry shrimp and pumpkin roti.

There was something about Trinidad that made my heart soar. Something about the sun and the sea and the sand and the people and the culture just made me feel happy and free. Since I taught phys ed, I spent that year in shorts, a T-shirt, and flip-flops or a pair of sneakers. On weekends, Xavier, Holly and I went to Maracas Beach. We drove the windy, winding North Coast Road, always stopping at a pullover spot to stock up on my favourite snacks: tamarind balls—which are bite-size taste bombs of tamarind, hot sauce, salt and sugar—and a delicious sweet-hot concoction called mango chow. Then we took in the breathtaking view of the lush cliffs overlooking the Caribbean. At some point during the day, we took a stroll from the beach over to the food trucks in the parking lot to replenish our beer supply and make a mandatory stop at Richard's Bake & Shark to pick up an order of the Trini version of a Big Mac. Just swap the burger for boneless shark meat; the bun for deep-fried flatbread; the ketchup, mustard and mayo for pepper sauce, cilantro, garlic, tamarind and mango chutney; then top it all off with pineapple slices instead of a pickle and ditch the fries for a side of slaw. Coupled with an ice-cold Guinness or Stag beer, it was pure heaven. That year I also started dating Dion, a local teacher at the school, and we went island-hopping to Grenada and Saint Lucia. We took in soccer and cricket games, attended jazz festivals, hiked through lush forests leading to secluded beaches, explored farmers markets and taste tested all the local beers while watching spectacular sunsets. Pure bliss.

A special electricity fills the air during Carnival time. Wherever you go, infectious calypso and soca beats and rhythms blare from big trucks carrying steelpan orchestras and monster sound systems. Carnival Monday and Tuesday and Mas (short for masquerade) are the big parade and costume days. Tens of thousands of masqueraders, adorned in exquisitely designed costumes festooned with feathers, sequins and beads, fill the streets. People jump to their feet, sway to the music and dance in the street, making friends, sharing food and drink and revelling in the shared joy of the Carnival spirit.

Nighttime is especially magical. The streets sparkle with colourful lights, and festivalgoers celebrate at fetes (organized parties) featuring popular soca artists and headlining bands. That year I was even more euphoric than usual because a bunch of my friends had come down and we'd put them up at our house. I spent the entire time in a state of elation, dancing and partying in the streets and at party venues around town, surrounded by people I loved. It was one of the freest, most exhilarating experiences of my life.

And yet despite the awesome year I was having, it wasn't long before I began to feel the winds of change blowing again. I loved the students, but I'd grown bored with teaching and had started to chafe at the regimentation: the bells, the bureaucracy, the schedules. Also, I was thirty-two by then, and I wasn't banking any money. My path was financially unsustainable. And I couldn't go on partying for the rest of my life. I realized I'd come to another crossroads and began thinking about what shape my life would take next.

I thought back to the parts of teaching I'd loved most. The times I'd always found the most rewarding were when I got to hang out with kids after school in the phys ed department. I thought back to how much I'd always loved teaching in that pilot program at Emery and talking to the kids about their lives. I decided to see if there was some way I could parlay those pieces into a new career. I explored social work, psychology and psychotherapy, and I landed on psychotherapy.

I knew I didn't want to enroll in a program that would require me to attend classes at a physical college or university every day. I wanted to find an online program that would allow me to pursue my studies while I travelled the world. I found one at Seton Hall University in New Jersey that met all my requirements. Seton Hall was a good school with an accredited program. If I enrolled in it, I could earn my master's in counselling psychology and all the credits I needed to become a practicing psychotherapist. I applied to the program and was accepted, and that spring I gave notice at the international school. Initially, I planned to fly home when our house rental lapsed at the end of term, but then I realized I loved it there. Why not just stay in Trinidad, rent a house and do the course down there?

I went home for the summer, lived with my parents, and returned to Trinidad in the fall. Holly and Xavier didn't come back that year, so I rented a house with Lauren, a friend with West Indian roots whom I'd met through mutual social circles in Toronto. We rented a furnished house in a gated compound where a couple of my Trinidadian friends lived. The compound was across the highway from the one where Holly, Xavier and I had lived the year before. The area was decent, although less affluent and a bit rougher than the one where we'd lived the previous year. The compound, like most in the island's more upscale areas, was well protected. All the windows had bars, and all the bedroom doors had locks. All the houses had two doors—an outside gate made of metal bars and the wooden front door of the house. Having two doors allowed occupants to leave the wooden door open to let in fresh air during the day while locking the exterior metal gate. When you locked up, first you padlocked the exterior metal gate. Once you were inside the house, you turned your key in the doorknob and locked the front door behind you. Each time, without fail, I made sure to lock both the metal gate and the wooden door.

I began my master's course in September. Between attending online lectures, doing the required reading and completing assignments, I had to put in five or six hours a day. I mentioned earlier how I'd always chafed at studying and doing homework when I was in high school. Well, I didn't exactly change my ways afterwards. I did zero reading when I was at teachers college, and I skipped all my academic classes when I was in university. My coach knew I didn't always go to my classes, and he told me that if my grades started to slip, he'd have to send me to study hall to bring them up. But I managed to keep them up, and he never had to send me.

After I started at Seton Hall, however, all that changed. For the first time in my life, I liked learning. I inhaled the required readings, and I was so fascinated by the ideas and theories we were studying that I began googling to learn more about them. I was so enthralled I didn't even mind sitting! I learned about the work of Dr. Irvin Yalom, a renowned psychiatrist and psychotherapist who profoundly influenced the understanding and practice of psychotherapy. I learned about Aaron Beck, who pioneered cognitive behavioural therapy, and John Bowlby, whose work on attachment theory is pivotal to our understanding of how early relationships and attachment affect our development. I learned about various psychoanalytic treatment approaches; differences in the ways men and women develop; Adlerian theory; gestalt therapy; mood, eating and sleep disorders; and on and on. For the first time in my life, I encountered an academic field of study and thought, *This is my thing.*

Lauren and I turned out to be compatible roommates. Mornings, after awakening and having coffee, we usually went for a run and then sat down at our respective computers to work. She was working virtually for a Toronto-based insurance company that year. After work, we met up for dinner, then either hung out at home and watched TV or saw friends. Weekends, we headed to the beach, hung out with friends and partied. I wasn't dating Dion anymore—we'd broken up the previous spring—so I was a free agent.

In November, I learned that Ulpia, a friend from Toronto, was headed down to Saint Vincent with her boyfriend to visit family, so I decided to jump on a plane and meet them there. We stayed on the mainland with her aunts and uncles for a couple of days, went to the beach, drove around the island with one of her uncles, then took the ferry to Bequia, a small island off the coast of Saint Vincent, where we stayed with another of her family members for a couple of days and hung out at the beach. I had my laptop with me and did my coursework while I was away. We were gone for five days. When I returned, I was ecstatic. Having the spontaneity to pick up at a moment's notice and just take off was so liberating. *This is the life*, I thought. As long as I have my laptop with me, I can go anywhere I want, whenever I want. No rules. No bells. No bureaucracy.

One night, not long after I returned, Jason, a lovely local guy I'd met at a party earlier that fall, came over for the evening, and we sat outside on the front steps talking and having a beer. He left around eleven o'clock. Lauren had gone to bed earlier, so after Jason said goodbye, I locked up, tossed my keys on the dining room table and went upstairs to bed. A few hours later, I was jolted from sleep. Two masked gunmen, their faces covered with bandannas, burst through my bedroom door, turned on the light and said, "Don't look, or we'll kill you." For the next two hours, they took turns raping me.

PART TWO

AFTER

Chapter Six

PICKING UP THE PIECES

I was lying in a fetal position on my parents' bed. My mom and Odia were trying to spoon-feed me soup, but food revolted me. I couldn't stand to have anything in my mouth. All I wanted to do was sleep. For the first month, sleep is mostly what I did. Often, I slept for ten hours at a stretch. No matter how long I slept, I awoke exhausted. At first when I awoke, my only goal was to try to make it through the next few hours. To do this, I tried to pick a few activities that would get me to lunchtime and a few more that would get me to dinnertime. I told myself if I just picked one thing I used to do, like get out of bed or smile at something I used to smile at, my parents would know my pilot light hadn't been completely snuffed out. I didn't fake it. I didn't have the energy to fake it. I just tried to do one small thing that would lessen their pain.

Some days, the grief was too heavy for me to carry. Some days, dragging myself out of bed to brush my teeth was more than I could manage. Others, I couldn't make it up the stairs to the spare bedroom on the third floor of my parents' town-house without collapsing in sobs on the second-floor landing. I told myself that even if my progress was minuscule, every day I survived would be one day further away from the nightmare I'd lived through.

***

When the men burst through my bedroom door and threatened to kill me if I looked at them, I put a blanket over my face. I'd pulled it from under my pillow. I've had it ever since my childhood. I can't sleep without it. I take it with me wherever I go. It was in my backpack when I went to Thailand. It survived the tsunami. After I covered my face, the men asked if there were any men in the house. They warned me not to lie. If I lied and a man surprised them, they would kill us both. I said I didn't think so but that my roommate went to bed before me, and her boyfriend might be staying over. I said to check the driveway. If there was a truck in the driveway, he was in the house.

I heard them go to the window. I heard them rummaging through my things. Then I think they went downstairs because I didn't hear any noises for a while. After some time had passed, I heard footsteps on the stairs. Then they came back into my room and began raping me. They were in my room for a long time. Then it got quiet. It was quiet for a long time. I didn't know if they'd left for good or had just gone downstairs and were coming back. I lay there frozen with the blanket over my face, paralyzed with fear, not moving a muscle. The only sound in that room was the sound of my teeth chattering uncontrollably.

When the sun began to rise, Lauren came into my room. *Oh my god,* she said. *That was so scary.* She knew someone had been in the house who should not have been in the house. But she didn't know what they had done to me. She crawled into bed with me. I told her what had happened. *Oh my god, Sara. Oh my god. Oh my god.* We lay there side by side, mostly in silence. Sometimes we talked about what to do. I was too scared to call the police. The men had said if I called the police, they'd come back and kill me. We knew two Canadian teachers who lived in a complex nearby. We decided to drive over to their place once the sun rose and confer with them. Once the sun came up, we knew it would be safe to go.

About six thirty, we drove over to our friends' complex, woke them up and told them what had happened. We debated about calling the police but were too terrified. I called Dion, the teacher I'd dated the previous year. Dion was a local. I thought maybe he could advise us. Dion told us to call the police. He said the men were gone and weren't coming back. The police rarely caught the perpetrators. The men would have no way of knowing if we'd called them. We deliberated a while longer, but in the end decided calling was the right decision. We called, then drove back to the house to meet the police there.

I tried calling my parents, but I couldn't reach them. It was still too early in the morning. I tried calling Odia but couldn't reach her, either. One of my teacher friends kept trying my mom. Eventually, she reached her. She told her what happened, then handed the phone to me. *Oh my god, oh my god, are you okay?* my mom kept saying. *Yes, I'm okay,* I kept responding. This wasn't true. I was far from okay. As far from okay as it's possible to be and still consider yourself a member of the human race. But what else could I say?

The police had to bring some equipment into the house, but it was raining that afternoon, and when it rains in Trinidad, everything grinds to a halt. It took the police a while to get their act together. Eventually, they brought their equipment inside and marked my bedroom as a crime scene. They

numbered and took pictures of the evidence. They asked us
what the men took. We told them what was missing: our wal-
lets, cell phones, a camera, an iPad and some jewellery.

The police asked me a lot of questions—the same ones
again and again. "Are you sure you locked the front gate?"
Yes, I'm sure. "Are you sure you locked the front door?" *Yes,
I'm sure.* "What did you do with your keys?" *I threw them on
the dining room table.* "Who was the last person you saw last
night?" *Jason was the last person I saw. But Jason didn't do this
to me. Jason is a good man.* The police had no interest in me or
in what I'd been through. In their view, what had happened to
me was routine. They told me matter-of-factly that if I weren't
white, the men would have killed me.

Nobody could figure out how my attackers had gotten into
the house. The question confounded us all. When I'd locked
up the night before, I'd locked up the same way I did every
night. I shut and padlocked the metal gate. Then I went inside,
turned my key in the doorknob, locked the front door behind
me, tossed the keys on the dining room table and went upstairs
to bed. But when Lauren and I went downstairs the following
morning, the front door was wide open, and there was no sign
of a break-in, which meant the men must have had keys to get
inside the house. The only theory the police and I could come
up with for how they got inside was by inserting a pole with a
hook on the end of it through one of the barred dining room
windows and fishing my keys off the dining room table.

The police wanted my clothes for evidence. I was desperate
to shower, but I couldn't shower or give them my clothing until
I had gone to the hospital and had a forensic examination. I
wasn't sure I wanted to have one. If I had a forensic exam, then
what? Dion had told us the police rarely made arrests in these
cases. If the police did find and arrest the perpetrators, there'd
be a trial and I'd have to relive the horror. I didn't see any good
options.

In the end, I decided to go to the hospital and have the examination done. It was the only agency I had in the situation, my only way of holding those men to account, whether they were ultimately held to account or not. The Canadian teacher couple drove us to the hospital. It was a Sunday morning. When we arrived, only a few staff members seemed to be working. Nobody could locate the rape kit. The nurses called around and tried to track it down. I stood at the front desk, dissociated, trembling. I think it took around forty-five minutes until someone finally found the kit, but to me it felt like an eternity. A nurse led me into an examination room; I disrobed and lay down on the exam table while she took swabs from my body parts and bedclothes. When she finished, she handed me the morning-after pill and told me that when I returned home to Canada, I needed to get tested for HIV.

Afterwards, we had to go back to the house. It was the last place I wanted to be, but I knew my mom and Odia were flying in later that afternoon to bring me home, and I needed to pick up a few things. The Canadian couple drove us over. I went inside, threw a few things into a bag and left. I didn't want to be in that house one second longer than I had to be. Dion drove us to the Hyatt. I was numb, affectless, a dead woman walking.

By the time we'd checked in and I'd showered, it was almost the end of the day. By then I had a killer migraine. My head was throbbing so relentlessly I asked Dion if he'd massage my neck. As he began the massage, I momentarily dissolved into the sweet feeling of relief, then recoiled in disgust at the touch of a man's hands on my body. Dion felt horrible. I felt horrible. I knew he was just trying to comfort me.

My mom and Odia flew in late that afternoon. The next morning, we went to the airport. Then yet another waiting game. We waited for the plane to arrive. We waited for the staff to get their act together. We waited for the flight to board. When we were finally on board, my mom handed me an

Ativan. I had never taken a sedative in my life, but I swallowed it without argument. In that moment, and maybe for the rest of my life, all I wanted was oblivion.

***

As soon as I returned home, I had to get tested for HIV. My mom drove me to the clinic. I had to wait for the results. A few days later my doctor called to say I was negative. As a preventative treatment, I had to take a course of antiretrovirals for a month, then get tested every three months for a year. Only then would I know if I was in the clear. Every morning, I had to swallow two tablets the size of horse pills. I was supposed to take them with food, but I was barely eating. The pills made me so nauseous on an empty stomach that I retched every time I had to get them down.

Shortly after I was back, I started seeing a therapist I'd gone to a few times before I moved to Trinidad. I'd begun seeing a therapist before I moved down because I wanted to understand why I kept breaking off relationships once they started to become serious. Odia and Eva now shuttled me to and from my various appointments.

During our therapy sessions, I told my therapist what I was feeling, even though what I was feeling was numb. I told her things I couldn't tell anyone else. I was having nightmares. Terrifying nightmares. I was afraid my dad would think I was tainted and would never see me as beautiful again. I wished people would stop asking me questions. Questions like *How did the men get in?* and *Are you sure you locked the gate?* and *Why aren't you angrier at them?* I knew, like me, they just wanted answers. I knew they were just trying to manage their feelings of helplessness and rage. But their questions felt like interrogations, their anger like judgments. And I didn't have room for their feelings. I had enough of my own to process. I told her that after what those men did to me, I couldn't stand to have anything in my mouth. That while they were raping me they kept saying how strong and beautiful I was, and now I didn't want to do anything that might make me feel strong or beautiful. Like work out or wear formfitting clothes. I refused to wear anything but baggy sweats and wouldn't shave my legs.

I was filled with an overwhelming sense of shame and self-reproach. I blamed myself for the break-in. How could I have been so stupid and careless as to toss my keys on the dining room table? I blamed myself for being so compliant during the attack. I just lay there the whole time and went along with everything the men wanted to do to me. I didn't even ask them to please stop. Why didn't I scream or put up a struggle?

Exactly four weeks after I came home, it was Christmas Day. Everyone tried to make the best of the situation and pretend it was a normal Christmas. But there was nothing normal about that Christmas, and everyone knew it. Somehow we made it through the holidays. Afterwards, I could no longer bear to live under my parents' roof. As much as I love my parents, living with them filled me with despair because it was a constant reminder that my life was on hold.

Before I was raped, I thought of myself as a resilient, adventurous soul. Not even a tsunami, a thief with a knife to my back or flying bullets could destroy my openhearted wonder about the world. But Trinidad was different. Trinidad crushed me. My sense of safety and self were suddenly snatched from me that night, and I didn't know if I would ever get them back. I didn't know if I would ever feel safe when I closed my eyes at night again. I didn't know if I would ever find the courage to travel again. I didn't know if I would ever feel joy again—or if I would be condemned to live out my days with this hole in my heart. I had to start living life on my terms again. I had to see if it was possible to reclaim what those men had stolen from me.

In January, I rented an apartment in Toronto in a new condo

building near the midtown streets of Yonge and Eglinton. The building had twenty-four-hour security. No one could get in or out without checking in at the front desk. My apartment was bright and modern, but the round-the-clock security sealed the deal. I moved in on the first of February and began trying to return my life to some semblance of normalcy, even though nothing about my life felt anywhere close to normal. I was like a wounded veteran readjusting to civilian life. I had to relearn everything: how to sleep alone, how to trust my instincts, how to laugh and feel free again.

Odia offered to sleep over the night I moved in, but I declined. I was determined to get through that first night on my own. I thought of toughing it out alone that first night as a gift to myself. I knew I had an upward climb ahead of me. But if I could make it through the first night alone, I would have taken my first step. Rationally, I knew I was safe. I was in a big condo building with front desk security. I had an alarm in my unit, and the alarm was on. But nothing about trauma is rational, and when it was time to go to bed, I was scared. I fell asleep with the TV on and my bedroom door closed. I got up a few times during the night to check the front door and make sure it was locked. Then I let it be. I had nightmares, but none so bad that I couldn't fall back to sleep. I woke up at five o'clock in the morning and watched a movie until the sun came up. Then I congratulated myself. *You did it*, I told myself. *You made it through.*

Next, I established a daily routine. By January, I'd resumed attending online classes. When I'd told my professor why I'd suddenly vanished from classes, he'd credited me for any uncompleted coursework. I'd already handed in most of my assignments and it had been almost Christmas by then, so I hadn't missed much. Mornings, I walked to the local Starbucks with my laptop to do my schoolwork. When I finished my schoolwork, I went for walks in the neighbourhood, wandered in and out of stores, listened to music and went to my medical and therapy appointments.

At the end of February, I heard friends were heading to Barbados for five days, and I decided I wanted to go with them. I made this decision over the vocal objections of my parents, brother and every single one of my close friends, all of whom thought I'd lost my mind. Nobody could fathom how I could even consider returning to the Caribbean. Ever. What they failed to grasp was the depth of my pain and sadness in not knowing whether I would ever feel safe enough to return to a part of the world where I'd once felt so gloriously alive.

As much as I wanted to go on the trip, I was apprehensive. I tried to remind myself that I was travelling with people I knew, we were staying at a safe hotel, and this was Barbados, not Trinidad. Still, for the first couple of days, I was agitated and constantly on guard. I took a catamaran boat cruise with friends and spent time with Jason, who came over from Trinidad to see me. Little by little, I settled down.

By March, by all outward appearances, I was making progress. Living alone: check. Doing my coursework: check. Travelling again: check—albeit with chaperones. But inwardly I was plagued by a constellation of symptoms I was powerless to control. I was scanning for threats all the time. I had brain fog, headaches and gastrointestinal issues. I had invasive thoughts and memories throughout the day—some triggered flashbacks. When I had a flashback, I started hyperventilating. I had frequent nightmares. If I had a nightmare or heard a news story about a break-in or sexual assault, my system went haywire. I also experienced this weird, tingly, butterflies-in-my-stomach feeling in my legs and feet and sometimes in my arms and hands. When the feeling manifested in my legs or feet, I had the impulse to move or flee. Usually, the trigger was witnessing an altercation or someone jostling me on the street. But sometimes the feeling came on for no apparent reason.

In the months prior, my therapist had provided me with a safe space to express my feelings and validated them without judgment, which was exactly what I'd needed. By March, though, I realized that I needed a more specialized kind of treatment. I googled "Toronto trauma specialist," which was how I found myself in the office of sensorimotor psychotherapist Sandra D.

Sandra was a slender fortysomething woman with a calm, confident manner. During our first session, she told me that her approach to treating trauma was holistic, based on the mind-body connection. Trauma doesn't just affect the mind, she explained. It also leaves a mark on the body. Sensory experiences, physical sensations and the way the body reacts to trauma all play a significant role in how someone processes and heals from it. For trauma survivors, learning to become aware of the energy we all have stored within our bodies, and how to release it, is a safe way of revisiting the trauma. By involving the body in the therapeutic process alongside the mind and emotions, it's possible to provide a path to healing that goes beyond talk therapy alone. If I could become more attuned to my body's sensations and movements, I could start to release the physical tension, stress and pent-up trauma trapped within it. During our sessions, Sandra would work with my body's energy and employ various techniques and exercises to help me become more aware of it and learn to better regulate my body's responses to trauma.

And so began the next leg of my uphill climb.

Chapter Seven

THE LONG ROAD BACK

For the next year and a half, I saw Sandra twice a week for therapy sessions. During our work together she introduced me to various concepts to help me understand what was going on in my body. One was the window of tolerance. She explained that we all have this idea of a window of tolerance within us. We might deviate or move a little up or down within our window depending on how our day is going and what is happening, but most of the time we live in the middle. In the middle, we're emotionally balanced and feel safe, calm and present. In the middle, we're engaged and alert; we can think and respond clearly, handle life's challenges and function optimally; and our emotional reactions equal the magnitude of what's happening to us externally.

The window of tolerance was particularly relevant in my case, she said, because trauma narrows your window. If you don't have a history of trauma, and something triggers you in your day—like maybe someone jostles you on the street—you take it in stride. But with trauma, your window shrinks to a sliver, and it doesn't take much to make you jump far outside of it. Even though a stranger's accidental bump is not a threatening situation, your nervous system doesn't know that, because it can't distinguish between your present circumstances and your past trauma. Instead, that innocent jostle triggers a flashback that causes your system to think you're in danger and react as if you're being chased by a tiger in the grasslands. Once it detects danger, it prompts your fight-or-flight response to kick into overdrive and flood your body with hormones such as adrenaline and cortisol. You then enter a hyperaroused state of emotional reactivity: your heart rate spikes, your palms sweat, you become jittery, you have trouble concentrating, and you may even start to panic or become enraged.

Likewise, if you have past trauma and find yourself in a situation that is so overwhelming that it's beyond your ability to handle, your nervous system reads that situation as dangerous as well, but in that case, you drop far below your window and go into a freeze state and your body starts shutting down. Your body temperature lowers, you dissociate, and you become emotionally numb and freeze or feign dead, in the same way that a mouse plays dead to improve its chances of escaping with its life when a cat has it cornered.

In the normal course, our bodies should be able to cycle through the ups and downs of daily life. In the normal course, we should be able to live in a state of emotional flexibility. But with trauma and a narrowed window, the body's responses can get stuck at a high pitch, causing a person who has been traumatized to become riddled with anxiety all the time, or alternately to become so overwhelmed that they can get stuck at the low end in lethargy and depression so severe that they feel utterly dissociated and can't get out of bed.

During our sessions, Sandra did energy and somatic bodywork with me. She taught me exercises to help me become aware of my body energy and how to release it. In one exercise, I had to concentrate on where I was holding the energy and what it was telling me to do. Then, right there in her office, I had to perform the motion it was directing me to do. If it was directing me to kick, I had to kick. If it was directing me to get up and run, I had to get up and run. If it was directing me to punch, I had to punch a pillow.

She also taught me mindfulness exercises and ground-ing techniques to help me recalibrate my emotions and bring myself back into my window of tolerance. We worked a lot on these grounding and stabilizing strategies at first, to make sure I was able to bring my body back to a sense of safety and presence. This was far from easy at the beginning, but I be-came well versed in the strategies, often begrudgingly so, since practising them was exhausting. The more I practised, she explained, the wider my window of tolerance would ex-pand, which would build my capacity. She taught me how to breathe to calm myself and plant my feet on the ground to an-chor myself. If a memory caused me to become flooded with anxiety during one of our sessions, she'd calmly tell me to start breathing, look around the room, and name some things I could see, smell or touch to remind myself where I was and that I was safe. She had me smell essential oils and eat a sour candy to help reorient myself back to the present. She had me push against a wall for fifteen seconds, then shake my arms out to rid myself of any excess bodily energy and gradually re-store balance to my nervous system.

She explained that parts of the brain can encode traumatic memories. When I had flashbacks, my brain was recalling them and I was reexperiencing them. But when the brain recalls memories, they can become malleable, which intensifies their emotional charge. The good news, however, is that the brain is a highly plastic organ, so I could influence my emotional asso-ciations with those memories. Cognitive behavioural therapy

(CBT) and eye movement desensitization and reprocessing (EMDR) are particularly helpful in that regard, and at different points during my recovery process I tried both. But she also explained that I had another option—an even better one, in my view, because it afforded me complete creative freedom to rewrite the script for the horror movie playing in my head.

If I engaged in positive new experiences, I could influence my memories to create positive new emotional associations to compete with—and potentially override—the negative ones residing in my brain. In other words, if I didn't like the movie streaming in my head, I could replace my current trauma-ravaged associations with my memories with lighthearted ones by going out and doing something that would allow me to create joyful new associations with that memory and in essence rewrite the script.

She also helped me reframe the narrative I'd been telling myself: that the attack was my fault. She said my belief that I was somehow responsible for it because I threw my keys on the dining room table and didn't try to flee or fight back wasn't objective truth. It was just a story I had been telling myself. When my body realized it couldn't fight or flee, its only way of surviving was to shut down and go into a dissociative freeze state. Since the brain is so elastic, if I told it a different story, I could rewire it to react differently. We talked a lot about how I could begin to challenge the story I'd been telling myself by flipping the script. Instead of viewing my passivity as a sign of weakness, I could view my body's impulse to freeze during the ordeal as a survival mechanism.

We also talked a lot about where self-compassion fits into the picture. She had me perform some hand-on-heart self-compassion strategies. I had to place my hand on my heart to evoke warm, comforting feelings meant to provide me with a sense of reassurance. I repeated self-soothing affirmations, telling myself I was worthy of love and understanding, I was doing my best, and it was okay for me to struggle. I hugged myself and stroked my arm and face to nurture myself and help release tension. I composed a self-compassion phrase and repeated it whenever I started berating myself for causing the attack.

Sandra also had me write down my thoughts and feelings, including a compassionate letter written to myself as if I were writing it to a friend: acknowledging my struggles, expressing understanding and offering words of encouragement. Then she led me through a series of exercises to help me reframe the narrative. Partly the goal of the exercises was to take me back in my mind to a point seconds before the traumatic event and help me become aware of what my body *wanted* to do to survive in that moment—but couldn't. Once I traveled to that point mentally, I had to react the way I wished my body had reacted physically. In that way, I could rewrite the ending of the story to make it comport with the ending I wanted. During our sessions, I had to practice getting up off the couch and walking out the door, but instead of freezing and going numb, I had to run, push and punch. As she'd explained when we first met, the therapeutic exercises she had me do were designed to train my body to rid itself of the energy to fight or flee that was stifled during the attack. I dutifully did these exercises, and others, every time we met. But for a long time, I thought they were patently ridiculous.

The work was intense, and many times I left Sandra's office mentally, physically and emotionally exhausted. Often, I left enraged. I didn't have to endure just two gruelling sessions of this therapeutic work per week. I had to do therapy homework every day. I had to practise mindfulness exercises to draw my five senses into the present moment to calm my system. When I went for a walk, I had to notice birdsong, rustling trees and foraging squirrels. I had to feel the wind on my face, notice the scent of a flower and take in the odors of garbage and gasoline.

I had to do this while taking deep breaths: five seconds in, seven seconds out. I had to practise breathing and humming. I had to breathe in for five seconds and hum on the way out. Apparently humming stimulates the vagus nerve, which is also a part of my nervous system but different than the part that controls my stress responses. If I hummed, breathed deeply and stimulated the vagus nerve, it would calm my nervous system, which would counteract the heightened stress responses the other part of my nervous system was causing.

I did as I was told. I practised the exercises daily. I practised because I was desperate to rid myself of my symptoms and because I was a good soldier. But it infuriated me that this was my life now. That I had to spend my time thinking about this shit.

After the sessions, I needed to decompress, so I put in my earbuds and wandered downtown listening to reggae and my favourite soca artists. I put in only one earbud, though, never two. I needed to stay aware of my surroundings at all times. Often, I went to an Ethiopian restaurant situated in an old house on Irwin Avenue that my cousin had introduced me to years before. It was a cozy spot and always felt like home to me. I'd known the owner, Mohammed, for years. When I arrived the first time, he greeted me warmly. I'd lost a lot of weight since he'd last seen me, and I looked emaciated. But he didn't ask any questions. He brought me a vegetarian platter, which he knew was my favourite dish. I tore off tiny pieces of injera bread, dipped them into the curried chickpeas, and for a few moments I felt at peace.

***

That spring, I resumed going out for drinks and to soca parties with my friends. They knew how on edge I could get in a crowd, so whenever we were at a club or in any crowded situation, they formed a protective circle around me, especially the guys. It was like having my own Praetorian Guard. That spring I also resumed playing sports. That year, for the first time ever, I took up winter running and began putting in close to forty-five kilometres a week. My only way of distracting myself from my daily physical and emotional suffering was to sprint up hills and focus on the excruciating burn in my quads instead. By the time summer arrived, I was ready to resume working out in a serious way. More than anything, I needed to feel strong again.

I returned to the gym and began working out with a personal trainer. I connected with one of the guys on staff there, and we wound up having a summer relationship. When we connected, I made the conscious decision to be intimate with a man again. I chose him deliberately. I could tell he was a good guy. I knew where he worked. He was not some rando. I was almost defiant about it, like when you decide to lose your virginity and get it over with. Even though he knew my history, I trusted that he was a decent man, and I was the one calling the shots. I had no idea how my body would react. But I was unwilling to have the experience of intimacy with a man stolen from me. The only way for me to override the last memory I had on file was to create new associations with it. The experience wasn't optimal. But for me it was pivotal, because it reminded me of something I needed to remember: there are good men in the world, men like my father and brother and all my male friends—and my Spidey sense about the men I choose to let into my life was good and remained intact. It was one of the only silver linings of the entire soul-crushing experience of my assault in Trinidad and its aftermath, and I clung to it ferociously.

That summer there was also an opening in a ten-week group therapy program for survivors of sexual assault. I had learned in my master's course that group therapy can be a valuable counterpart to individual therapy if you've done individual work and come in with a set of helpful strategies. The group met twice a week in a large second-floor space near Kensington Market. Ten or fifteen women, ranging from late teens to late middle age, sat around in a large circle sharing their stories, while two therapists guided the session. I was the only person in the group who was white and middle class. I was also the only participant who didn't know her attackers. Most of the other assaults had taken place within the context of intimate partner violence.

The participants could choose whether to share their stories or not. I didn't share mine, partly because I didn't like talking in front of groups, but also because I'd had so much therapy that I didn't feel the need. The course covered a lot of the same ground I'd already covered in therapy, so I didn't get much out of it. Still, I was not sorry that I'd signed up. The sessions gave me an anchor for my week. Afterwards, I followed my usual routine and wandered around the city listening to music—one ear attuned to the harmonies and beat, the other alert to the sound of potential threats.

One afternoon after the session wrapped, I was on my way downstairs with one of my earbuds in my ear when a woman in the group—fortyish, jeans and a sweatshirt, nose ring, covered in tats—followed me downstairs and asked me where I was going. I told her I was going for a walk and to listen to music. She didn't take the hint that I wanted to be alone, and when I got to College Street, she kept walking beside me. Hoping she would get the message, I said, "If I don't decompress after the sessions, I struggle for the rest of the day and night."

"Yeah, I know what you mean," she said. "But you don't really look like someone who's been through hard things in life."

***

In August, I had to go to Seton Hall in New Jersey for five days of intensive lectures, classes and evaluations. The campus was gorgeous, and I found the lectures riveting. Suddenly, all the readings I'd been doing came to life. I got to know my classmates, found it exhilarating to spend time with like-minded people embarking on this exciting new career together, made a bunch of new friends and came away feeling I had a brand-new community.

I'd been busy logging air miles since my trip to Barbados in February, so I no longer had fears about travelling alone. Since then, I'd been to San Francisco with my brother, London with Odia, and Singapore and Thailand to visit Roxy and my friend Shauna. (That last trip was a big deal for me because it was my first time travelling such a long distance alone.) But as great as it felt to have my travel mojo back, I still hadn't conquered my white whale.

Despite all my work with Sandra, whenever I thought about returning to Trinidad, I became immobilized with fear. At the same time, I was profoundly sad about what my fear said about everything I'd lost. My grief was compounded by the fact that I'd missed going to Carnival with all my friends that year. I'd gone to Carnivals somewhere in the world since my late teens. But once again, as terrified as I was at the thought of returning, the thought that I might never return was worse. I knew the only way I'd ever find out if I could conquer my fear was by going back and seeing for myself. I decided it was time.

My family went ballistic when I told them. I understood their reaction. If I were them, I would have been furious, too. But I wasn't them. I was me, and I had to face this dragon my way. They knew me well enough to know that once my mind is made up, I'm not inclined to unmake it. *Well, you know Sara. This is what she does,* they would say when I announced a decision they thought was off the wall. Still, I wanted their support and blessing. I needed to know they were behind me and would back my decision. We had a family meeting. The only way they were willing to get on board was if we established some ground rules. Number one: my mom and my brother, Travis, would go with me. (My dad had made it abundantly clear that he would never set foot on that island again.) Number two: we would stay at the Hyatt.

Before the trip, I was deeply torn. Part of me felt horribly guilty for putting my mom and Travis in a position where they felt that their only choice was returning to a place they detested and had caused them unfathomable pain. At the same time, I was enormously relieved and grateful they'd agreed to ride shotgun on the trip because I couldn't imagine doing it without them.

When the plane touched down, I was swamped with bad memories. It was rough. Really rough. But having family at my side bolstered my courage, and when the cortisol rushes started, I went to my grounding strategies. During our stay, we invited friends over to the hotel and visited with friends and former colleagues at the international school. Everyone knew my story. It was all over the news when it happened. Rape may be a common occurrence in Trinidad, but when it happens to a foreign white woman, it's headline news.

During that trip, my feelings oscillated wildly between a disorienting sense that nothing about the island felt the same anymore and a cathartic, empowering feeling that I had made it back and was walking on Trini soil again. Part of me was bereft knowing that I would never live in Trinidad again—or be free of having to manage my trauma symptoms when I returned. But another part felt enormously proud of myself for achieving such a major milestone. I knew I still had another huge challenge ahead of me—one that would require summoning even more courage—and that was returning for Carnival. Then I would be with friends, not family, in and out of Trinidad more, hanging out in crowds a lot and staying out late at night. But this was a win—a big win—and I took it. In December, I logged another significant milestone. For the first time in a year, I gave myself permission to feel pretty again and I shaved my legs. As I slid the razor along my right calf, I noticed how easily it glided across the spot where I used to have the gash from the tsunami wound. In seven years, that wound had closed, and scar tissue had formed over it. For a long time, the scar tissue protruded above the surface of my skin. But I noticed it had melded into my skin and now blended seamlessly with the landscape of my body. I stared at the smooth, flat surface of my skin and marveled at how what was once a deep, angry fissure was now just a part of my story. *Wow*, I thought, *it takes time, but eventually, wounds heal.*

Chapter Eight

BACK IN THE GROOVE

I headed into the next year feeling I'd done everything I possibly could to lay the foundation for rebuilding my life. I was back to doing virtually all the activities that, for me, made life worth living. With Sandra's help, I had gained a basic understanding of my nervous system's role in triggering my trauma symptoms and had mastered strategies to manage them. If I'd had a jarring experience even a year earlier, I would have been flooded with intolerable feelings. Now if that happened I might start to deviate slightly beyond my window of tolerance, but not so far beyond its borders that my nervous system would think I was being chased by a tiger and either panic and run or think *WTF?* and freeze. That was tangible progress, and I congratulated myself for having achieved it. At the same time, I was deeply aware of what it had taken me to get to that point and knew I could not possibly have done so without the support of my friends and family, who had stood by me unwaveringly. I don't just mean by offering me their emotional support, although of course that was crucial—I mean their financial support as well. For trauma doesn't exact just a high psychic toll. It exacts a significant economic one, too.

My therapy sessions with Sandra cost $145 an hour and weren't covered by provincial insurance. I considered her treatment worth every penny, but my parents were the ones footing the bill, and it wasn't lost on me that I could not possibly have afforded to pay for my treatment on my own. I knew I was incredibly lucky to be in that position. Now that I'd finally begun to feel like a human being again, I promised myself that when I became a therapist I would pay it forward by doing pro bono work with sexual assault survivors and hold spots in my practice for those who couldn't afford to pay for treatment.

Still, despite all the progress I'd made, I knew I wasn't on the other side. I clenched my jaw so often it ached and so much when I slept that I cracked a tooth and had to get a nightguard. I still experienced jittery feelings in my arms and legs at times throughout the day, and I still struggled with terrible thoughts, memories and nightmares. Whatever tripped the wire in my nervous system, the result was always the same: cascading rushes of cortisol and adrenaline. Many days, my ongoing symptoms were so demoralizing that I despaired of ever feeling like myself again. But there was nothing to do but keep pressing forward.

Fortunately, in February I had something else to focus on: Carnival. It was coming, and this time I was going. That trip I had another goal besides just returning to Carnival with my friends. I was determined to go back to the house where it had happened. The house that Lauren and I had shared. In my mind, returning to Trinidad for Carnival wasn't just about creating a new memory of Carnival. It was also about creating a new memory of the house where I was sexually assaulted. That house was situated close to a main road, and it was a road we always travelled when we were on the island. Unless I had a happier memory of it, every time I drove down that road, I'd remember what happened to me there and be afraid.

I had the whole scenario planned out in my head. Lauren and I would go back to the house together and share a Guinness. Sharing a Guinness was central to the enterprise. It had to be a Guinness. I associated drinking a Guinness with happiness. It was my favourite beer, the brand I almost always drank on the island and the one we always kept stocked in our fridge. Jason would drive us over. Jason, with whom I'd shared a Guinness as we sat talking on the front steps the night before.

I told my plan with Lauren before going down. We figured that between the people, parties and parades, Friday was our best shot. The day came and Jason picked me up first, at the Hyatt. I was staying there in compliance with family rules. Then he picked up Lauren. On the way over, I began to tremble and feel waves of nausea. I didn't fear that it was dangerous to go back to the house. It was the middle of the day, and I was with friends. I was worried that returning to the scene of the crime would trigger such an intense trauma reaction that it would ruin the rest of my Carnival fun. On the drive over, I silently talked myself down: *You can do this. You can do hard things. Look how far you've come.* As we pulled up to the house, I felt myself start to panic, struggle for breath and begin to dissociate. But I just kept telling myself, *This is your choice. You're here with friends. This is now, not then.*

Jason parked the car and stayed back to give us some privacy. Lauren and I walked over to the house and stood outside for a while, sipping our beers. Then I wandered around to the side, looked up at the second-storey bedroom window and said a little prayer of gratitude for life, the love that surrounded me and the fact that I no longer had to live in fear. Afterwards, I walked back to where Lauren was waiting, and we finished our beers. In that moment, I felt a beautiful lightness, as if the immense, staggering weight I'd been carrying for so long had finally lifted, and at last I could entertain the possibility that maybe, just maybe, I was free.

Carnival was sublime. I had moments that threatened to knock me off balance, but that was to be expected, and by then I knew the drill. If an upsetting memory showed up and threatened to derail me when I was swaying my hips to the music or conversing with someone I hadn't seen for ages, I didn't get angry. I looked around, reminded myself where I was and told myself I was safe. Then I got lost in the music again.

*＊＊

For the balance of that year and the following, finishing my master's degree was my main focus. To earn my degree, I had to accumulate a certain number of supervised clinical hours with an accredited organization. In the spring of 2013, I secured an eight-month placement at Evergreen Drop-In Youth Shelter. Evergreen has since changed its name to Evergreen Centre for Street-Involved Youth and has moved locations, but at the time it was on Yonge Street just south of Gerrard, in the heart of downtown. Starting in May, I shuttled between Evergreen and the nearby Yonge Street Mission building a few times a week.

Evergreen was a happening place. It had a hot bar where kids could come in off the street and get a hot lunch every day, and a recreation area with benches around the side where they could shoot pool, play table tennis and hang out. Downstairs there was a computer room and two career counselling offices. My supervisor and I conducted therapy sessions in a small room off the recreation area. In many cases, the teenagers and young adults we worked with were unhoused either because they were unwelcome at home or because the street was a safer place for them to live.

One of the reasons I had applied to work at Evergreen was

how much I'd loved working with my Emery students. Just as I had in that case, I found a way to connect with the Evergreen kids on a human level. I had a knack for knowing how to speak their lingo without sounding like a phony or coming across as someone who'd parachuted in from another world and was trying too hard to ingratiate herself. The fact that I was well travelled gave me some insight into their lives, and because of my struggles, I was able to empathize with them as well as admire how hard many of them were working to turn their lives around.

One summer afternoon I was standing at the corner of Jarvis and Gerrard waiting for the light to change when a guy in a hoodie riding his bike on the sidewalk came whizzing by me from behind and grabbed my cell phone right out of my hand. I was so stunned that it took me a minute to realize what had happened. As soon as I did, every alarm bell in my body went off. The incident would have been upsetting for anyone. But it was especially retraumatizing for me given my history, and doubly so because it was a sneak attack from behind. Worse, it didn't happen when I was travelling in a developing country. Or at night. It happened in broad daylight on a busy downtown thoroughfare in my own city. If it could happen in my own city, there was no safe place anywhere.

I was so freaked out by the experience that I couldn't return to Evergreen that afternoon. I had to go straight home. Afterwards, my post-traumatic stress disorder symptoms returned with a vengeance. The incident was a real setback, and it took a few months for my system to shake off its impact. Before it happened, I'd always taken the subway downtown. I still took the subway, but now I felt uneasy travelling on it. I was afraid to take out my phone while I was in transit, and I had a running commentary in my head the whole way. My only way of calming my nervous system was talking myself through my anxiety: *Is this going to happen to you again? Is something else going to happen? It's possible but not probable. No, you're okay.*

After that incident, I never felt the same way about Evergreen again. Even in the best of times, Evergreen was an unpredictable place. Some kids were drunk or high on drugs. From time to time, fights broke out. Before the man in the hoodie stole my phone, I could handle the unpredictability. But suddenly, Evergreen felt like a much more uncertain place to me, and I spent my days there in a state of high anxiety. I finished out my hours but never really enjoyed going back after that incident. I never felt the same way about going downtown again, either. I was always on edge, always wondering what was coming around the next corner, and eventually, I stopped going. After that incident, wandering around downtown listening to music was over for me.

***

In September, after spending three years working towards my master's, I earned my degree, graduated and officially became a psychotherapist. Before the course wrapped, we had one last class to say goodbye to our classmates and exchange personal notes. I'd shared my story with them during our time together. In their notes, several told me how much they admired my courage for sharing, especially given my shyness. Others expressed admiration for my quiet acceptance of the ordeal and determination to just go on in the face of all I'd endured. Their words touched me deeply. In my darker moments, when I need to remind myself how far I've come, I turn to them for solace and encouragement.

I had another graduation that month: my graduation from therapy. After a year and a half, I believed that I finally had the tools I needed to manage my trauma. Now it was my turn to help other sexual assault survivors learn how to manage theirs. I'd been thinking about what shape my practice would take for a while. By the time I graduated, I had a vague sense that I wanted my practice to be trauma focused. I didn't know exactly what that meant yet. I just knew I wanted to draw on my personal experience to help others cope with trauma. In the past few years, I'd developed a basic understanding of trauma and how to treat it. I still had tons more to learn, of course, but I was keen to educate myself.

One of my supervisors had told me that you can't work exclusively with clients who have been through trauma or you'll burn out. I knew I'd have to balance my practice with clients that therapists refer to as "the worried well"—ones who tend to come in with more garden-variety issues related to marriages, relationships and careers. Those problems are important, too, of course, but listening to stories of that nature all day doesn't affect you in the same way that listening to stories of sexual violence and abuse does.

I had to start somewhere to launch my practice, so I set up a profile on the Psychology Today website and rented a four-hour block of office space from a clinician who worked in my neighbourhood. Slowly but surely clients began to reach out, and before I knew it, I was in business. I went into the office from nine to noon on Mondays, began with one client and built my practice from there. I was still struggling with a fair bit of anxiety after the bike incident, so I wasn't as proactive as I ordinarily would have been about calling clinics to ask if they needed a part-time therapist. Every couple of months I also took professional education workshops. The College of Registered Psychotherapists of Ontario requires you to do a certain amount of professional development each year to be certified and retain your license afterwards. But I also took workshops on subjects that interested me, like narrative

therapy and cognitive behavioural therapy, because I was trying to figure out what I wanted to specialize in.

By the end of 2013, I finally felt like my old self again. After
a series of struggles and backward slides over the three years
prior, I was firing on all cylinders and felt fully back in charge
of my life. I was having fun, laughing a lot again, engaging in
all the activities that gave me joy, and doing so without second-
guessing myself, which was huge. I was eating normally again
and no longer had to break my food into morsels just to get
it down. I was able to return to Trinidad when I wanted, and
when I did, I felt the same sense of joy and ease I'd always felt
when I was there. I still had unpleasant memories and flashbacks, but they'd dwindled to occasional occurrences, no
longer threw me off my game the way they once had, and increasingly receded into background noise in my life.

When I'd first started with Sandra, I didn't know anything
about trauma, and it would be many years before I truly understood the theories she introduced me to—or why I needed
to understand them. But the knowledge she imparted to me
was invaluable. She effectively handed me a user manual for
my nervous system, and with her guidance I started to shift
the lens through which I viewed my sexual assault. I hadn't
completely stopped blaming myself for what I viewed as my
complicity in it, but she helped set me on the path to taking
my story back. Another reason I was so happy that year was
because I was fully back into athletics. I was running, working out, playing sports and in tip-top shape. That summer, I
was invited to try out for Team Canada's national ball hockey
team. I didn't make the cut—I enjoy playing ball hockey, but
it's not really my game. However, the Italian team was allowed to take one foreign player to the tournament, and I got
the gig. The tournament was held over ten days in St. John's,
Newfoundland and Labrador. We played almost every day. It
was intense. But when I'm in peak shape I feel invincible, and I

came out of that tournament on top of the world. Three years earlier it would have been inconceivable for me to imagine getting to a place where I felt hopeful and invincible. But that is how I felt. It was official. I was back in the groove.

Chapter Nine

BRAND-NEW LIFE

The following year I continued to build my practice and work towards accumulating the supervised and one-on-one client hours I had to accumulate to become a fully registered therapist. To that end, I began putting in a few hours a week at Dr. Roz's Healing Place, a shelter for domestic violence survivors. The hours I worked with women at the shelter counted towards my final accreditation as a registered therapist, but my primary reason for volunteering my time was to make good on my promise to myself to give back when I became a therapist. That year, I also began volunteering at the Forgiveness Project, a nonprofit that helps trauma survivors focus on reconciliation and healing. I spoke to students and community groups and contributed a personal essay to a book of survivor stories published by the organization. Aside from wanting to educate and help others, sharing my story helped me feel that maybe some good could come from my experience.

That year I began thinking a lot about having a child. I'd

been thinking about having one on and off since my early thirties, when all my friends started to get married and have kids. I was thirty-six years old by then, and I felt as if a big chunk of my thirties had been stolen from me. My fertility window was also starting to close. After I finally emerged from the dark tunnel of those past few years, I began asking myself what the next five were going to look like. The one thing I always knew about myself—and knew with absolute certainty—was that I wanted to be a mother.

I started thinking that if I was going to have a kid, first I'd have to meet someone who wanted one, then I'd have to fall in love with that person, then I'd have to get to the point where I wanted to spend the rest of my life with them. The odds of that happening seemed slim to none. Not just because my fertility window was about to snap shut but because even if I did manage to find and fall in love with someone, I'd still have to be willing to commit to spending the rest of my life with them, and that was a Rubicon I'd never been able to cross. It began to stress me out every time I started going down that rabbit hole. To lessen my stress, I decided that if the pieces didn't fall into place by the time I was thirty-seven or thirty-eight, I could always take matters into my own hands.

That summer, all of this was in the back of my mind when one of my former Emery students invited me to attend the birth of her baby. The experience was life-altering for me. I distinctly remember leaving the hospital after witnessing the birth and thinking I simply could not miss out on that experience myself. No matter what it took, I would never let anything stand in the way of becoming a mother. A couple of months later I was sitting in the office of a fertility specialist.

The doctor and I exchanged pleasantries, then she asked me why I'd come. I explained that I was at a crossroads in my life. I knew I wanted to have a kid, but I wasn't with anyone. Should I wait to meet someone? Or have a child on my own?

She looked me in the eye and posed a question I will never forget: "Sara, if I told you that you can only have one of those things for the rest of your life—you can have a baby and become a mother or you can have a partner to grow old with—which of those options would you choose?"

It took me less than a second to respond. "Become a mother," I said.

"Well then," she said, "if you know for certain that being a mother is a life experience you don't want to miss, then why would you wait to act on that choice, especially when there's a time window on it?"

I knew right then and there I was going to go ahead. What she said made so much sense to me. Her question was so clarifying that I use the same technique whenever I have a big decision to make. I also use it with friends and clients when they're grappling with a big decision. Nowadays, it's quite common for women to have kids on their own, but at that time I didn't personally know anyone who'd made that choice, and I needed a bit of hand-holding. "Do women do this? Am I absurd for doing this?" I asked the doctor. "Are you kidding me?" she said. "Many, many women are making this choice. You have no idea how many. You are one hundred percent not alone."

"Okay," I said. "Let's do it."

She explained that there were no guarantees that intrauterine insemination would work, since age, health and various other factors can impact success rates. But given my age and the fact that I was in good health and shape, the chances were good. Then she walked me through the process. A reproductive endocrinologist would assess my medical history and do some tests to determine if IUI was a good option for me. If so, I'd choose a sperm donor from an online donor registry and pick a date for the procedure. Since timing is crucial for success, the clinic would closely monitor my menstrual cycle, track my hormone levels and perform ultrasounds beforehand to pinpoint when I was about to ovulate. On the day, the donor sample would be processed in a lab to remove impurities and increase the chances of fertilization. The procedure itself was relatively quick and minimally invasive. I'd lie on an exam table, a thin, flexible catheter would be inserted through my cervix into my uterus, and the sperm would be carefully injected. Afterwards, I'd have to lie down for a short while to allow it a better chance of reaching the egg. Then I'd have to wait for two weeks before taking a pregnancy test. If the procedure was successful, a fertilized egg would implant in my uterus. If not, I could continue to undergo the procedure until it implanted. If I wanted to go ahead, all I had to do was pick a start date. I told her I wanted to get started in the new year.

I always knew that if I decided to become a single mom, I'd want to include my parents in the process. I'd vaguely mentioned to them that I'd been thinking about pursuing IUI. Whatever they thought about my decision, or whatever worries they might have had about how I'd manage on my own, I was confident they'd be happy about it. They know I don't do well when options are taken from me, but more than that, I believed the fact that I was making such a life-affirming choice would signal to them that I was in a good place, and I hoped that would trump any other concerns they might have.

After I saw the fertility doctor, I told them I'd decided to go ahead. They took a beat to absorb the news, but then, just as I'd anticipated, they said, "Okay, maybe this is a little unconventional, but it's such a Sara thing to do, and we're so happy to see you moving on with your life, and we're going to be grandparents! So yeah, we're all for it!" That Christmas I flew out to Vancouver for the holidays. On Boxing Day, we were relaxing on the couch in their living room with a fire crackling in the fireplace when I asked if they wanted to help me choose a donor. Of course they were game. We each poured ourselves a glass of wine, I set my laptop down on the coffee

table, and we huddled around it and began going through pro-
files together. The experience was a lot like going on a dating
app. We'd land on a profile, look at the photos and read the bio,
and my dad would start nixing choices, often for completely
baseless reasons—or at least for reasons unrelated to the task
at hand. He'd say something like, "He's not good enough for
her," and my mom would say, "Oh, for the love of god, Alex,
she's not going to marry him. She's looking for a sperm donor!"
And then he'd realize we weren't in the market for his future
son-in-law, and he'd say, "Okay, okay," and we'd move on.

We made five or six picks that night, then narrowed the
list down to two. (You have to pick an alternate in case the
clinic runs out of sperm vials for your first choice.) The donors furnish photos of themselves from infancy to adulthood
and provide information about their heritage, medical history,
physical and personality traits, hobbies and various other details like their parents' and grandparents' careers. They also
write a letter about why they chose to become donors. Some
of the donors are open to the child contacting them when they
come of age. Others prefer not to be contacted.

My first choice had German and Irish heritage. (My mom
has Irish roots, and I wanted my child to have my heritage
and bear a resemblance to me, at least in part.) He described
himself as adventurous, athletic and musical, all of which
are traits I value. Mostly, though, I just thought he sounded
well rounded. But what ultimately clinched my decision was
his letter. His aunt had had a child on her own. He wrote that
watching her go through the experience and seeing how much
having the opportunity to become a mother meant to her had
inspired him to help other single women who also wanted to
become moms. I'd read a lot of donor letters, but none had expressed sentiments like his, and they moved me.

Soon the date for my first round of IUI arrived. I waited
for my cycle to kick in, had the blood work and ultrasound

done, then more blood work, and then they called me from the clinic to say the egg was ready. I went in the next morning, put on one of those hospital robes, lay down on the exam table and had the procedure, which was pretty much as advertised. The only glitch was that I'd failed to anticipate that lying on the exam table would trigger a flashback to lying on an exam table in the same position during my forensic examination in Trinidad. The situations were completely different, of course. I didn't choose to lie on that exam table in Trinidad—or at least I didn't choose the circumstances that led to my lying there—whereas I did choose to undergo the IUI procedure, hopefully to become a mother. My body, however, was incapable of making that distinction, and I lay there trembling, my heart pounding, throughout. The first round didn't take, but the deep sense of disappointment I felt when I received the negative result was a clear sign that I was on the right path.

The following month I returned for round two. That time, the procedure took. When I learned I was going to be a mother, I was elated. After so much suffering, finally, finally, my life was unfolding as it should.

Chapter Ten

FREEZE

I was going to be the person who worked out and played sports and traveled right up until my due date. I had it all planned out. But that's not exactly how things turned out. In March, I had a miscarriage scare. It was a false alarm, but I landed in the hospital and had to go on bed rest for a week. During my first trimester I had brutal morning sickness—so brutal I started dry heaving in the middle of conducting a therapy session at Dr. Roz's and had to hightail it to the washroom. There was no way I could keep working there, and in March I had to quit. It was during my fourth month, however—when my belly began to grow and the baby started to move—that things really started to go south.

I should have experienced the baby's growing presence in my body as a reassuring sign that I had a healthy, normally developing baby. But that's not what happened. Instead, as the baby grew, I felt as if I had a foreign object in my body. After what I'd been through, the notion triggered such intense feelings of fear, anxiety and revulsion that I became obsessed with getting it out. Only I couldn't. Worse, it was growing bigger and bigger every day. Instead of the feeling that I was nurturing another human being whom I couldn't wait to meet, I felt as if I were being consumed by one. I was living *Invasion of the Body Snatchers* in real time.

During the day, I was mostly fine. I went about my day, and it would periodically dawn on me that I was going to have a baby, and I'd stop and marvel at the wonder of it all. I'd think, *You're literally growing a human being inside of you. That's unbelievable.* In those moments I felt a deep and loving sense of connection to my baby. But then night came, and with it the panic attacks. My panicky feelings manifested as a heavy weight on my chest. Sometimes the pressure was so severe I thought I was having a heart attack.

My last trimester was a horror show. I couldn't get a decent night's sleep. Either the baby was kicking constantly or lying directly on top of my rib (which made finding a comfortable sleeping position impossible), or I had to pee. Once I was up, going back to sleep was out of the question. Then my anxiety started to spiral. I kept thinking this thing inside me was only going to get bigger and bigger, and I had no way to stop it from growing. There was no way out. It was like being trapped in an elevator. The panic attacks grew so bad, and I became so consumed with anticipatory dread, that I had to talk myself through what I'd do if an attack came on and I couldn't breathe. *If that happens, you'll just have to call an ambulance.*

I tried to manage my anxiety, but it was futile. Those last few months I was so terrified, demoralized and sleep deprived that I had to go back to Sandra for a refresher course on grounding and mindfulness techniques. She explained to me that pregnancy often triggers similar reactions in women with a history of sexual assault. We reviewed how to bring myself back into my window. She had me practise putting my hands on my belly and talking to my son. (I knew by then I was having a boy.) I had to walk around her office and tell myself, *You're just having a freeze response. That's just your son inside of you, the one you chose to have. He's supposed to move around. That's how you know everything's fine.* At night, when I felt him move and my anxiety started to spiral, I had to walk around my apartment, talk my body down, remind myself I was just having a flight response or sit in a bath, and when I felt him move, I had to breathe, hold my belly and say, *Oh, buddy, it's just you, moving again. You're a mover and shaker just like I was.* In effect, I was holding and hugging and calming my nervous system in the same way you'd hold and hug a baby to calm it down and let it know it was safe.

I trusted Sandra and the process because I knew it worked and had helped me before. But having to repeat the exercises felt ridiculous and enraging all over again. I was enraged at the men who'd done this to me. Who'd caused me all this suffering. And not just me. My son, too. I knew he couldn't be living inside his mother and not feel her pain.

My due date was the first of November. The day came and went. A week passed, but my water still hadn't broken. My doctor told me I could keep waiting for my water to break or I could be induced. I chose induction. I was huge and needed this pregnancy to be over. I went into St. Joseph's Health Centre the following day to have the procedure, then was sent home to wait for my water to break and told to come back when my contractions were coming regularly and a set time apart.

My contractions started coming on fast at five o'clock the next morning. I got to the hospital around eight. By the time I arrived, I was seven centimetres dilated. I was told I had to wait until I was ten centimetres before I could start pushing. The nurse asked me if I wanted an epidural. I said yes. My contractions were coming on fast and furiously. An hour or so later a nurse came into my room and gave me the epidural.

Then everything slowed down. In the room with me were my mom; a naturopath and doula I'd worked with during my pregnancy; and Cris, a woman I'd met playing ball hockey the previous summer and with whom I was in a relationship.

At some point that afternoon a nurse came into my room and broke my water. When my water broke, meconium came out. Meconium is the baby's poo. It's a thick, gooey greenish-black substance and a dangerous sign. If you see meconium, you have to get the baby out fast. Infection can set in. The baby can aspirate it during delivery and wind up with respiratory issues. The nurses told me to start pushing. I pushed and pushed but couldn't get him out. His head was too big. My contractions started coming on harder and faster. I didn't know that my epidural had started to slip out. Nobody knew. I began convulsing from the pain. The baby's heart rate started to spike. "We have to get him out right away," the nurses said. "You need a C-section. We have to get you into surgery." They rushed me into the operating room. No one was allowed to come with me. I could feel myself beginning to dissociate. They strapped me to the operating table, cuffed my hands and feet. I became hysterical, started fighting to get out of the restraints. "Please, please don't tie me down. I have a history of trauma. If you tie me down, you'll retraumatize me." The pain kept escalating. I kept convulsing. The nurses kept screaming at me to keep still. The next thing I knew, a mask was over my mouth. Then everything went black.

**

I woke up in recovery. A nurse came in and topped up my morphine. At three in the morning, another nurse came and woke me up. Your son isn't breathing well, she said. We have to send him to SickKids hospital. An ambulance is coming to pick him up. The medics will bring him to you before they transfer him.

The medics wheeled him to my bedside. I had to fight to keep my eyes open. All I saw was a tangle of wires and tubes. I felt nothing when I saw him. I reached out my pinkie and touched his hand. The medics took him away, and I drifted off into a morphine haze.

The next morning, I was still in pain, still going in and out from the morphine. A nurse came into my room and said I had to start pumping breast milk. I wanted nothing to do with pumping. She made me pump anyway. My dad and Cris ferried my breast milk to SickKids. The neonatal intensive care unit staff at SickKids gave it to my son through a feeding tube. My family came in and out of my room all day. They'd all been to see him in the NICU. *He's gorgeous! He's huge! Eight pounds, ten ounces. You've got to see him. You're going to love him so much.* But what if I don't?

He was born on a Tuesday evening. Thursday afternoon the nurses came into my room and said, "It's time. You have to go and see your son." I told them I didn't want to see him. Cris was with me. "It's okay," she said. "I'll go with you." On the way to SickKids I started crying. Everyone said I was going to love him, but I didn't think I would. The NICU was a cacophony of beeps and code reds. Nurses rushed around; babies wailed. A nurse pointed out his crib amid the sea of incubators. "That one's yours," she said. Again, all I saw was a tangled mess of wires and tubes. Again, I felt nothing. As far as I was concerned, he could have been somebody else's kid. The nurse asked me if I wanted to hold him. I declined.

I was discharged that day, but he had to stay in the NICU. I went to visit him twice a day. I went in the morning, stayed for a few hours, got home and napped, then returned for a few hours at night. Cris took me, waited for me and brought me home. She had taken time off work to care for me. I knew I was supposed to have feelings for my son, but I felt no connection to him. Sometimes when I went to the hospital, I held him.

Sometimes I didn't. Over time, I grew a little more comfortable holding him, but I still didn't feel anything. The nurses taught me how to bathe him, but bathing him felt too intimidating, so mostly they bathed him. What if I disconnected one of his wires or tubes? I was informed he might have meningitis and needed surgery. The doctors performed the surgery. They inserted a tube up his ankle into his heart and blasted him with heavy-duty antibiotics.

He remained in the SickKids NICU for two and a half weeks. After that, he still needed care but a less acute level, so he was transferred to the NICU at North York General Hospital. He stayed in that NICU for another two weeks. I continued pumping and visiting him twice a day. After Cris returned to work, I took taxis to and from the hospital. He was released on December 5. He could breathe on his own. He no longer needed wires, tubes or breathing apparatuses. But you could tell he was still working hard to breathe. He had a little indent under his ribcage that became increasingly recessed when his lungs were straining to push oxygen in and out. The nurses warned us to watch him closely to make sure the indent didn't become too recessed and his lips didn't turn blue. If they turned blue, it meant he wasn't getting enough oxygen. On release day, I was completely hands-off. Cris was the one who carried him out in his infant seat. Cris was the one who strapped him into the car. Cris was the one who watched over him to make sure his lips didn't turn blue.

After we brought him home, I did the things you're supposed to do to keep your baby alive. I fed him, I changed his diaper, I rocked him to sleep. But a lot of the time, I was just going through the motions. Sometimes when he smiled or we played, I felt joy and a connection to him, and in those moments it was as if the sun had emerged from behind a dark cloud. As the days went on, this happened increasingly frequently, and the feelings of connection grew. But mostly I remembered those ten months as a scary, lonely time. Either I was overwrought with anxiety or so dissociated I just wanted to sleep. I wasn't worried that I would hurt him. It was just that except for those welcome interludes when I was able to experience feelings of warmth and attachment, I felt detached from him and from life in general. What I was experiencing wasn't just the normal overwhelm of new motherhood, although that was certainly part of it. I was suffering from PTSD and postpartum depression brought on by the trauma of his birth.

They don't exactly send you home with a manual when you have a baby. You're supposed to know what you're doing. But I didn't know what I was doing. Not really. Most new mothers don't have a clue what they're doing, either, of course. What was different in my case was that I felt so little connection to my baby so much of the time that I resented having to care for him all day. I resented the endless pumping, which triggered bodily feelings I detested. I resented it when he started to scream every time I had to put him down to pump. I resented the endless bottle cleaning and organizing. I resented having to wrangle all the baby paraphernalia. Still, I performed these tasks. If I hadn't been required to perform them, all I would have done was sleep.

I was also lonely. I could make plans if I wanted. I had people I could see. But I didn't want to make plans. I didn't have the energy. Besides, what if the baby started screaming and I couldn't settle him down? He was not doing well, either, at least to my eyes. His breathing was still laboured. He still had the little indent in his chest. The doctors told me he was doing okay, his lungs would get stronger in time and the indent in his chest would go away, but I was fixated on the indent and his breathing, just as I was fixated on his lips, petrified they would turn blue. Sometimes my anxiety became so severe that

my head started to spin. The only way I could regain my equi-
librium was by putting him in the stroller and taking him for a
walk. I went for a lot of walks.

I also struggled with grief and rage, although "consumed"
would be a more apt way of expressing how I felt. I was intensely sad and bitterly angry that once again I'd been robbed.
Robbed of the chance to experience a normal pregnancy.
Robbed of the birth experience I longed to have. Robbed of the
chance to bond with my baby. I had no memory of my son's
birth. I was out cold the entire time. I hadn't had the chance
to see him being born or feel the warmth of his body on my
belly when he emerged from the birth canal. We'd never had
that skin-to-skin contact that triggers the body to release oxytocin, the bonding hormone. From my body's perspective, I'd
delivered a stillbirth. Then a couple of days later, the nurse had
handed me this baby with tubes coming out of him and said,
"Don't mind the way he looks." It was so far from the birth
experience I'd imagined and planned for, it was unbearable
thinking about it. And this time there was no way for me to
recover what I'd lost. This time, no matter how hard I worked,
I couldn't reclaim the experience. Rationally, I knew that having no memory of my son's birth wasn't the worst thing in the
world. I knew that many people live through far worse birth
experiences, assuming they're lucky enough to conceive at all.
Even within the context of my story of trauma, that loss played
such a minor part. And yet despite all the misery I'd endured,
it still pulverized me. I could not get past it. Like, how many
fucking traumas did I have to go through?

PART THREE

BEAUTIFUL ADAPTATIONS

Chapter Eleven

HEY, BODY, YOU'RE AWESOME

I called him Kaden. That's the name I chose for my son. I started researching names as soon as I learned I was having a boy. I had a short list. But Kaden was always my first choice. I liked the sound of the name. I thought its hard consonants lent it a feeling of strength. I thought it worked well with my surname. Mostly, though, what resonated for me about the name was its dual meanings: "companion" and "spirited warrior." I hoped that by bestowing the name Kaden on my son he'd grow up to have both a fighting spirit and a softer, gentler side.

In January, when he was a year old, he went to daycare three days a week. Once he was in daycare part time, I finally had the mental space to focus on building my practice. With everything else I'd had going on since becoming pregnant, I'd struggled to find that focus. The only progress I'd made during the two years prior was officially becoming a licensed therapist and adding four more clients to my roster.

I was seeing only eight clients a week at that point, so I wasn't earning enough to live on. After Kaden went to daycare, I took stock of my situation and decided to look for part-time work. Supplementing my income was only part of my motivation. As much as I loved my new career, the work was solitary, and I'd begun to realize that motherhood could be lonely at times. If I could find part-time work at a clinic, I'd increase my income, bring more social interaction and balance to my life and still have time to build my practice. I found a part-time opening for a therapist at a college that offered a training program for dental hygienists. Students who needed support could consult with a therapist as part of their tuition. I was hired, and in April I began going to the college two days a week, every second week.

It wasn't long before students were lining up at my office door. Virtually all of them showed up with the same complaint: they were working around the clock just trying to keep up with the demands of the program and being crushed by stress. The college had compressed their entire training into an eighteen-month period. They were spending eight to ten hours a day attending classes and labs and the rest of the time studying. During that year and a half, they had maybe a week off between semesters and four days off at Christmas. It was untenable.

The majority of students, virtually all of whom were women, were in their late teens to late twenties, and most were from out of province. For many, it was their first time away from home and their first time thrust into a big city. They could barely care for themselves, let alone cope with such intense, relentless pressure. A smaller percentage of the students were older—late thirties to midforties—and embarking on second careers. Some had been out of school for so long they'd forgotten how to study. Many were managing households and kids on top of their schoolwork.

As if that stress wasn't crushing enough, the program was intensely competitive. The students had very few chances to fail a test or exam and were under enormous pressure not to. If you failed, you were out. In many cases, their families had taken out huge loans to pay their $40,000 tuition. They were petrified of disappointing their parents and wasting their money. They were so terrified of failing, it was all anyone talked about when they showed up for therapy appointments. Some carried such shame and fear around failing that they were self-harming and having suicidal ideations.

The intolerable level of stress they were under had them on a perpetual emotional roller coaster. Either they were in a constant panic or so numb they could barely function. Their sleep patterns were messed up. They had trouble falling asleep, or they woke up in the middle of the night, their minds racing. Some were losing weight from the pressure. Others were over-eating to cope with it. Many had trouble reading and study-ing or couldn't concentrate during lectures and lab sessions, which only increased their anxiety. Still others were lonely be-cause studying was all they ever did.

Several students reported having panic attacks. When an attack came on, their hearts started to pound, they couldn't catch their breath, and they began shaking uncontrolla-bly. Those would be scary symptoms for anyone to deal with under any circumstances, but they were especially debilitat-ing in their case because the panic attacks came on in the lab with instructors looking over their shoulders, evaluating their manual dexterity handling instruments. Worse, once you have one panic attack, it's so terrifying that you live in dread of another one coming on, which only escalates your anxiety, and that's what was happening to them. On top of all that, the life issues they'd been forced to confront while attending the program—living on their own for the first time, struggling to meet familial expectations and on and on—seemed to put pressure on every past trauma or negative core belief they had about themselves.

Most of the students had never experienced such extreme anxiety before. They had no idea what was happening to them, and their symptoms were terrifying. If I wanted to help them, I had to learn what was causing them to have such extreme stress responses. My first priority, then, was educating myself about the impact of stress on the nervous system. Next, I had to translate what I learned in an easily understandable way to help them grasp what was going on in their bodies. Finally, I had to come up with a logical way of framing their symptoms and give them tools to manage and gain some control over them, as Sandra had done for me.

From a knowledge perspective, I was essentially starting from scratch. During my work with Sandra, I'd picked up a smattering of information about the body's response to stress and the toll it could take on the nervous system, especially if the person had a history of trauma. But she'd focused less on explaining *why* my body was reacting as it was than on helping me rewire its responses and teaching me some grounding and mindfulness-based stress management techniques. During my master's course, we studied modalities for treating anxiety, but we didn't focus on its causes. The only other relevant knowledge I had to offer the students was of some techniques on how to identify and reduce negative thought patterns and behaviours, which I'd learned in the professional development course I took on cognitive behavioural therapy. Even if I hadn't started working at the college after graduation, I would have had to broaden my knowledge base to become the best therapist I could be. But once students began streaming into my office and breaking down in tears because of the stress they were under, that need became pressing.

That spring I embarked on a deep research dive. I cast a wide net in the fields of psychology and neuroscience and read whatever I could find on trauma, anxiety, depression, stress and healing. I didn't just read books and journal articles. I took a half dozen workshops on treatment approaches. During that year and the next, I continued to immerse myself in the literature. The more my theoretical knowledge deepened, the more I began to understand that the chronic stress the students were under was putting more pressure on their bodies and minds than they could reasonably handle, and their symptoms were external manifestations of their bodies having to work overtime to adapt to their stressful situations.

Before I began researching, I knew that stress and anxiety were different: stress was a temporary response to a specific situation that usually resolved once the stressor was addressed, whereas anxiety was a more generalized, pervasive emotional state, not necessarily linked to an identifiable trigger, that could persist even when the stressor was gone. I didn't know, however, that the body perceived both as threats and that both triggered it to have stress responses. I also knew beforehand that trauma narrows your window of tolerance, but I didn't know that poor sleep, exhaustion and chronic stress could narrow it as well.

Little by little, the puzzle pieces began falling into place. I realized that after enduring months of chronic stress, the students were hovering near or above their windows of tolerance all the time. If they had to cope with any additional pressure—an upcoming test, for instance—their windows were already so narrow that their bodies simply lacked the capacity to tolerate one iota more. As a result, their bodies interpreted—or, more accurately, misinterpreted—that additional stress as a threat, and then they did what they were programmed to do when they perceived a threat: sprang into fight-or-flight mode. That, in turn, only ramped up their already panicky feelings and created so much anticipatory anxiety that they couldn't function. It was like a runaway train.

The more I delved into the neuroscience, the more it fascinated me. I like it when things add up, and it adds up. The body has good reasons for reacting as it does. There is a beautiful logic to the way it functions. It is so practical, so pragmatic. It just makes so much sense.

When I met with the students, first I reassured them that they were not alone and told them that many, many other students were coming into my office overwhelmed and in tears. Then I walked them through how stress—especially the intense, chronic kind they were under—was sending their sympathetic nervous systems into overdrive. The program's pressures, coupled with all the other issues they were managing, were enormous burdens for anyone to carry. Those burdens were putting unrelenting stress on their systems, but our systems simply aren't built to deal with such prolonged, unremitting stress, and their bodies were struggling to regulate in response to it. Their symptoms were manifestations of their bodies' attempts to adapt.

I walked them through the body's stress responses, just as Sandra had done for me: how when the body perceives a threat it triggers a fight-or-flight response, which causes our nervous system to release stress hormones such as adrenaline and cortisol, which spikes our heart rate and blood pressure, which in turn makes us feel jittery and anxious all the time. Or, when the nervous system perceives extreme danger or system overwhelm, it triggers a freeze response, which leaves us feeling paralyzed and numb.

I told them that when rabbits perceive a threat, their nervous systems also flood with cortisol, they become jumpy and watchful and their eyes start to bulge. Or they freeze, their bodies hunch and their ears flatten against their head. Once the threat passes, they flick their hind legs. Some researchers theorize they do it to rid themselves of their pent-up tension. (When I first came across that fact, I realized it was exactly what Sandra had taught me to do to rid myself of my contained bodily energy.)

I gave the students a mini science lesson on how various brain parts work in tandem to respond to stress. How the amygdala is the brain's threat detector and processing plant for emotions, especially fear. How the hippocampus is the amygdala's manager, controlling our response to fear, and a storage facility of sorts for learning and memory. How the prefrontal cortex is the CEO of the whole enterprise and oversees the brain's learning, reasoning and thinking departments. I explained that when we're under stress, the amygdala immediately starts sounding the alarm that danger is near, which triggers the brain to release neurotransmitters like dopamine and serotonin, which prompts the body to respond swiftly and decisively in a crisis. Meanwhile, the prefrontal cortex is busily working to modulate the activity of the amygdala, and that can influence how we perceive and respond to stressors and help us see the threat as a little less scary.

I introduced them to the window of tolerance and pointed out situations that would prompt them to jump outside of their windows and trigger a stress response. I explained that since their windows were already so narrow from chronic stress, their nervous system was either hypersensitive to the distress signals it was receiving or misreading them as a threat. But even though their system was probably reading the signals improperly—feeling nervous about an upcoming lab or exam, for instance, was no reason to send their bodies into full flight or dissociation mode—their bodies and brains were simply trying to adapt to what they perceived to be a threatening situation in order to keep them safe.

If they were having panic attacks, I reassured them that when their nervous system triggered the release of adrenaline and cortisol and sent them into a hyperaroused state high above their window, while the feelings might feel scary and awful, they weren't dangerous, and their fear would only worsen their symptoms and cause them to panic even more. The good news, though, was that their symptoms were their bodies' blinking red engine lights warning them they needed to pay attention and that they were right to seek help. Then I taught them some grounding and mindfulness strategies to help them reorient themselves back to a calm, safe state, move them back into their window of tolerance and manage their anxiety around tests and exams. I shared some of the strategies Sandra had taught me as well as a few others I'd picked up during my research.

On the days that I went to the college, I met with students every half hour for four hours straight. During that time, I repeated the same information, or a variation of it, again and again. The effect was like cramming for the SATs. The more I drilled the information into the students' heads, the more I drilled it into my own.

And then a strange thing began to happen. The more I talked to the students about their symptoms, the more I began to realize I was experiencing many of the same ones myself. I wasn't having panic attacks. But I was jittery and on edge a lot of the time and experienced ricocheting emotions throughout my day. I also realized I still had a lot of residual energy in my body. It struck me that my body seemed to be having trouble deciphering whether I was simply overtired or facing some kind of threat, and I was experiencing roller-coaster emotions due to a narrow window of tolerance.

This was a revelation to me, and at first the realization knocked me back. I thought I'd put my trauma symptoms behind me ages before. I'd had that brief relapse after the stolen phone incident, but I'd recovered quickly, and while I knew you could never really be completely cured of trauma, I did think

I'd been in remission long enough to be in the clear. And yet, as resilient as I believed myself to be, the more I talked to the students about their symptoms, the more I realized I wasn't in the clear at all. Not by a long shot. Everything I'd learned over that year and a half about the body's response to stress led me to the inescapable conclusion that the culmination of all the trauma and stress I'd endured for the past several years was simply too much for my system to tolerate and had finally just done it in. At first, when this realization dawned on me, I was like, *Are you kidding me? Eight years later and I'm still dealing with this shit? I am so done. Will this torture never end?*

But then my perceptions started to shift. The more I framed the students' stress responses to them in a positive light, the more I began to view mine that way as well. Something about absorbing all that theory and witnessing its tangible, real-world impact on the students' understanding of their distress profoundly altered the way I thought about my own. Listening to them recount their symptoms, observing them play out be-fore my eyes in my office, explaining to them what was hap-pening in their bodies, walking them through strategies to manage their anxiety around tests and exams, then actually seeing the strategies work—or at least give them comfort that what was happening to them had a perfectly logical explana-tion, and seeing the relief on their faces when they realized that it had one—helped me see my symptoms differently, too.

I thought about how hard the students' systems were working to protect them. Even though their bodies were mis-reading the signals, seeing the effort their bodies were putting in to keep them safe gave me compassion for my own body and respect for how hard it had worked and continued to work to protect me.

Once I began to connect those dots, my world changed. Instead of viewing my body as my enemy and hating it for the hell it had put me through, for the first time I began to think of it as my friend. Instead of detesting it for besieging me with symptoms I constantly had to monitor and fight, I began to see it as this magnificent machine designed to watch over me, and the strategies it employed to keep me safe as its brilliant and beautiful adaptations. I was so astonished and moved by the genius of those strategies, I began to honour it for keeping me safe from harm. Sometimes, when I thought about everything it had done to keep me safe, I felt like tipping my hat to it and saying, *Hey, body, you're awesome.*

I thought back to how despondent I was after Kaden was born because I had no memory of his birth. I remembered a conversation I'd had with my doula at the time. She told me that nobody had a perfect birth experience, and the trauma I went through was the last thing my system needed, but at some point, I would have to try and reclaim a part of that loss. It had been two years since Kaden's birth. And yet I still experienced that loss as deeply raw and painful, and I still hadn't been able to reclaim any part of it.

But now, for the first time, I was able to grasp why I'd begun to dissociate when everything started to go south and they strapped me to the operating table. I realized I had no memory of anything that happened before they put me out cold because my body didn't want me to remember those parts. Just as my body's immune system worked to defend against an invading foreign attacker, my brain, in particular the prefrontal cortex, reacted defensively by preventing me from remembering the details of such a traumatic experience. My system was already in trauma overload. Prompting it to dissociate was its way of guarding me from having to endure more pain.

I thought back to the tsunami—how I was washed away in the wave and fled up a hill with my injuries and was stranded on the island for three days, and how when I came home, I looked for exits in every room I entered. Suddenly, it all made sense to me. Suddenly, I understood that my hypervigilance was my body's way of helping to keep me out of danger and provide me with the information I needed to flee a dangerous situation if another one presented itself.

I thought back to the robbery in South Africa and how everything my body did instinctively when I was under attack was designed to help me fight off my attacker and survive: how it triggered my fight-or-flight response and flooded my system with cortisol, which prompted my liver to release glucose into my bloodstream and provide it with an immediate energy source; how it increased my heart rate and blood flow to pump more oxygen-rich blood to my muscles and vital organs to ready them for physical activity; how it dilated my pupils to enhance my visual acuity and allow me to have a heightened perception of my environment; how it widened the airways in my lungs to facilitate my oxygen intake and optimized my respiratory function; how it sent oxygen and energy to my muscles to allow them to tense up and prepare me for quick, powerful movements and put me into a heightened state of readiness for physical activity; how it diverted resources away from nonessential functions such as digestion and immune system activity to prioritize my immediate survival needs; how it activated my sympathetic nervous system to increase my mental alertness and focus; how it temporarily suppressed my perception of pain and allowed me to continue functioning; how it caused me to sweat more to help cool my body during physical exertion.

Every single one of my body's adaptations collectively prepared itself for a rapid and intense response to the perceived threat. And then, once the threat had passed, it activated my parasympathetic nervous system to promote relaxation and recovery and return it to a state of balance. It didn't happen right away. I was jittery and on guard for a while. But it happened. The sheer magnificence of the body's beautiful adaptations took my breath away.

And of course I thought back to Trinidad, when I disso-ciated to survive. My nervous system responded to my terror in that situation by immediately flooding the zone with neu-rotransmitters and hormones and putting me into a state of paralysis. It put me into that state to disinterest my predators and improve my chances of getting the hell out of there alive. Then it protected me even more by making it hard for me to remember details like sights, sounds, smells and actual feel-ings and allowing me to recall only snippets of the experience.

It was only after I grasped the magnificence of the adapta-tions my body had developed to protect me from harm—and only after I began to revere and embrace them—that I truly began to heal. It was only after I understood the incredible lengths to which my body had gone to keep me safe and alive that I was finally able to forgive myself for not fighting back during the sexual assault. That was the turning point for me. That was the moment I truly began to move forward.

PART FOUR

NOW

Chapter Twelve

FORWARD FOREVER

In the spring of 2011, the year I was hell-bent on taking my life back from the brink after Trinidad, Odia and I went to London. The main reason we went was to see a soccer match. Arsenal Football Club, the premier team in the English soccer league—and Odia's favourite soccer team in the world—was playing a match in London that April, and we were able to score tickets. But we also wanted to go because Odia had purchased a brick in my name in Emirates Stadium, the club's home, in honour of my thirty-third birthday that April. She'd had it engraved with the words *FORWARD 4EVER*, the brick had been installed, and we wanted to see it together.

I've thought of those words often these past many years. In many ways throughout this journey, they have been my north star. Without them to guide me, I don't think I would have been able to keep going. At first, they took me only as far as lunchtime, then dinnertime and the second-floor landing of my parents' town house. But every day I kept them front and centre in my mind, I inched a little farther, and now, after all these years, here I am.

I took part in a ten-kilometre Spartan Race not long ago. Spartan Races are gruelling. Real Navy SEAL stuff. You have to wade through mud runs, do army crawls under barbed wire and climb ski hills with fifty-pound sandbags on your back. I know crawling under barbed wire with a lead weight on your back isn't everyone's idea of fun, but it is mine, and after the race, when a friend texted me a photo that she'd taken of me all covered in mud, my first thought was about how happy I am when I feel strong and how glad I was that I'd signed up for the race. But then I had another thought. It occurred to me that the kind of strength you need to compete in a Spartan Race is easy for me. That kind of strength I have. But the physical and mental fortitude you need for a Spartan Race is nothing compared with the kind you need to deal with the legacy of trauma. Living with the legacy of trauma is like walking around with a ten-ton weight on your back every day because trauma leaves an imprint on the body that never goes away.

For survivors, living with that burden becomes so much a part of their everyday lives that it's sometimes easy to forget how much effort it takes to shoulder it. One of my treatment goals when I work with trauma survivors is to help them realize how hard they're working to carry that weight every day. During a psychotherapy session, sometimes one of them will tell me a story about how they have to be on guard all day, and I'll say something like "Wow, that sounds so exhausting." When I make that observation, they invariably exhale, sink into the couch with relief and say something like "Oh my god, yes! *That's* why I'm so tired all the time."

Bearing that burden is so much a part of my own life now that I, too, sometimes forget the monumental effort it takes to carry it every day. It's usually only when I'm working with clients that I remember I'm shouldering a burden that others don't have to. Even with all the advantages I've had—a strong foundation, a loving support system and tons of therapy—I still have to carry it around with me everywhere I go. Trauma is a great leveller that way.

For instance, my attackers wore bandannas. During the pandemic, seeing a man wearing a bandanna as a mask instantly catapulted me into the red zone. I haven't seen any men wearing bandannas since 2022, but if I were to see one tomorrow, the sight would instantly elicit the same reaction. I don't think I'll ever be free of that.

Bandannas or not, I still have to deal with trauma triggers every single day. I have a running commentary in my head daily that I can't mute. It's there when I go for a run on the Beltline Trail near my house and see a man coming towards me from the opposite direction. It's there when I step into an elevator and see a man standing inside, and the elevator door shuts and it's just the two of us. It's there when a man passes me in a stairwell. When I'm in situations like those and others like them throughout my day, my first thought is always the same: *Is this guy going to attack me?* As soon as I have that thought, my body immediately registers a potential threat and I do a mental calculation to evaluate it. It's only after the threat has passed—the man goes by me on the trail or exits the elevator or leaves the stairwell—that I exhale and tell myself, *Nope, you're okay.* Sometimes I have to talk myself through that exercise when I'm sitting in my driveway at night before I get out of my car.

I recognize that most women have to reckon with a version of that internal dialogue at various times. The difference for someone who has endured trauma is that it's always there, like an app running in the background of their computer, using up too much RAM and slowing it down. One morning not long ago I went for a run along the Beltline. The Beltline Trail is my favourite place to go for a run in the city. I took our golden doodle, Jericho, with me. I wouldn't dream of going for a run in the Beltline without Jericho.

As I was running along, this guy began yelling obscenities at me. The obscenities were the standard misogynistic vitriol an incel would hurl at a woman or post about one online. It took me a whole day to recover from that incident. Another time a man jumped out of the bushes and startled me. My first thought was *Do I look pretty? If I look pretty, he's going to attack me.*

I've accepted that this is just the way it is for me now. On good days, I handle the cards I've been dealt in the same way I imagine people who have to live with a chronic physical illness handle theirs. On bad days, depending on the day and my frustration and exhaustion level, I become defeated or enraged.

Managing trauma requires ongoing effort. I still see a psychologist monthly to help me deal with past issues and cope with life's ongoing ones. I also have a supervisor in private practice. When one of my clients' stories triggers me, as they sometimes do, I seek guidance from her. When I come across stories or quotes that resonate with me and validate my experience, or when I find strategies I want to try, I add them as notes in my phone so they are handy and I can consult them whenever I need to. I also send content to friends and family members when I think they might benefit from the lessons and insights.

People sometimes say that trauma has made me stronger. That is a fallacy, and it frustrates me when I hear people say it to me or others. Trauma does not make you stronger, nor did it strengthen me. What trauma did for me was make me desperate to find some way to make its unbearable fallout stop. After years of effort, and at great expense to my parents, I learned strategies to beat back the memories and flashbacks and all the rest, and those strategies helped me and continue to help me. But they didn't cure me, because trauma isn't curable.

Manageable, yes. Curable, no. The effort I had to put into learning the strategies I needed to cope with the repercussions of the traumatic experiences I've lived through forced me to divert my attention from other areas of my life where I would have much preferred to put my focus. But putting in that time and effort was the only choice I had. It was my only way of re-gaining my sense of safety and self, my only hope of reclaiming my life and living it fully and joyfully.

The strategies helped me, and they continue to help me, even though many days they're not up to the task. But even if they were—even if they made all my symptoms go *poof* and I never had to deal with one more symptom again for the rest of my life—having those strategies in my arsenal does not mean that trauma has made me stronger. The effort I had to put into developing them, all of the crawling over crushed glass, has nothing to do with strength. It's the opposite of strength because having to spend your days in survival mode is pro-foundly enervating.

Where I do find solace and strength is by looking for mo-ments that provide me with a sense of gratitude and peace. One I've found is thinking about the men who give me space. When I walk down the street or go for a run or step into an elevator, I've noticed that some men can be extremely inten-tional about giving me a wide berth. Sometimes they smile and say, "Have a great day." It's as if they are silently acknowledging that they know my story, even though of course they don't. It's as if by giving me space they are telling me they understand, and even though it would never cross their mind to hurt me, and in fact they would rush to my aid if they saw another man trying to, they implicitly recognize that their gender alone can feel threatening to a woman. I think of those men a lot. I speak about them whenever I give talks. I am profoundly grateful to them. They make a huge difference in my life. Every time a man does that for me, he reminds me that not all men are a threat and that I can be safe in the world. That is a gift, and one for which I am profoundly grateful.

Another way I've found strength is by reminding myself of all the progress I've made. At first, when a man would approach from the other direction in the Beltline, I had to work my ass off to bring my system back down. Now I normalize much more quickly. I use strategies such as taking deep breaths to activate my vagus nerve and calm my nervous system or doing a quick "orienting to the present" exercise by using my five senses. In the early days, when I thought I'd have to live with bad memories for the rest of my life, I was disconsolate. Some trauma survivors are never free of their bad memories. But now when those memories come, they last only momentarily, and they no longer send me into an intolerable frenzy.

I'm also much more inclined to notice and appreciate every aspect of my life now than I was before. I know that's a cliché and what people always say when they survive a near-death experience. But I think it takes a brush with death to truly value life in all of its beauty and complexity. Coming to a deeper understanding and appreciation of life in all of its terror and glory, suffering and joy, has given me a much deeper understanding and appreciation of what it means to be human. And that has helped me rejoice in and embrace life again.

Humour has helped me heal, too. Having a sense of humour doesn't change your reality, but it can change the way you perceive it, and sometimes perspective is everything. When my clients tell me how exhausting it is to have a running commentary in their heads all day, I tell them to think of all the noise like a barking Chihuahua. It will have much less power over them that way.

I have also found it healing to write down my thoughts and feelings every day. Sandra encouraged me to engage in the practice to help shift my internal narrative from one of victimhood to one of empowerment, and it was helpful to me then.

I've continued with the practice, and it has turned out to have another unexpected benefit: providing me with a record of the arc of my recovery. I think of regularly recording my thoughts and feelings as my "trauma Fitbit" because it allows me to track my progress over time. Now when I look back at some of my earlier writing, it's clear I was in denial and trying very hard to convince myself that I was fine.

All the writing I've done and continue to do, including writing this book, helps to keep me moving forward. By setting down my story, I can control the narrative. By sharing it with others, I can find meaning in it. I can also determine if any good has come from it, and indeed, some has. Seeing how much my family and friends gave of themselves to help me come back from hell has been moving beyond words—and it has galvanized me even more than I already was to help those who have suffered as I have and advocate for those who lack my support systems.

Writing has also helped me think about my story differently. I used to view what happened to me as a violent breach of my true destiny, a perverse deviation from the happy life I was promised and destined to enjoy. Now I think of what happened simply as a part of my life, and of the future that unfolded in its wake as the only future that was available to me. We all have our tales of grief and abandonment, loss and despair. They're part of the human condition. I've learned that hiding from that fact and living in bitterness and rage will only hurt me.

To move forward, I had to find my way to forgiveness. Forgiveness, of course, isn't something you can achieve by snapping your fingers. It's a choice. You have to *choose* to forgive. Then you have to inch your way towards it gradually over time. It takes a lifetime to achieve forgiveness, I think, and finding my way to it has been my greatest challenge. It took so much time because there were so many things I had to choose to forgive. I had to forgive myself for tossing my keys on the dining room table. I had to forgive myself for not fighting back. I had to forgive the men who did this heinous thing to me. I don't mean their actions. I will never forgive their actions. Their actions are unforgivable. I mean that I had to work hard not to let whatever happened to them in the past— that had so blighted and damaged them that they felt entitled to rape me—continue to have a hold over my present and future. I allowed them so much power over my life for such a long time that in the end I felt I had no choice but to let them go. If I didn't let them go, I would have had to live the rest of my life with them at my side, and I knew I couldn't possibly carry that weight. To forgive, I had to get to a place where I understood that while I had choices taken from me that night, from that day forward the rest of the choices were mine. The moment I realized I still had choices was the moment I truly began to live again.

After I found forgiveness, I wrote a poem: *Finally her scars no longer screamed of rage nor fear/ but rather a freeing silence/ I forgive you/ I forgive me.* I had those words tattooed on my back. I had them literally seared into my body. I wasn't pretending when I wrote those words. Or when I got the tattoo. But just because I have forgiven doesn't mean that some days I don't still get angry. That some days I don't still say, *What the fuck? Why did you have to do this to me for a stupid robbery?* Despite the distances I have come, I'm still constantly forced to reckon with the question "What is healing, really?"

***

The greatest healing force in my life, bar none, has been Kaden. He, more than anything else, has helped me recover, because after he came into my life, I had something in it that was bigger than the trauma. When I look at him today, it's unfathomable to me that there was ever a time when I wasn't completely be-sotted with him.

As of this writing, he's nine years old and the epicentre of my life. He's funny and smart and super athletic. He does all kinds of sports: soccer, hockey, golf, swimming, you name it. Like me, he can pick up a new sport easily. He has a wicked sense of humour—really witty and sarcastic—and big, big emotions. He's a Scorpio, so he swings quickly from one emotional extreme to the other. He isn't musical in the sense that he plays an instrument, but he loves music and knows the lyrics to every song he listens to. Right now "Cold" by Maroon 5 and pretty much any tunes by Justin Bieber and Red Hot Chili Peppers are on his playlist. Lucky for me, he's a real cuddler. He's also incredibly sweet with animals and little kids. People love him. He brings light wherever he goes.

He knows he's the child of a donor. I've been very open with him about all that. He knows he can contact his donor if he wants, when he's older. He's aware of some parts of my history. He knows I was in the tsunami. He's seen the footage. It's like a movie to him. He doesn't know about South Africa. Or Trinidad. He knows he was very, very sick as a baby, but he doesn't know about the birth trauma or attachment piece. Sometimes I talk to him about resilience and the idea of the body's beautiful adaptations, but indirectly. He has a subscription to *National Geographic Kids* magazine, and one day we were flipping through the pages and looking at the pictures of animals, and we started talking about how they adapt to protect themselves from predators in the wild. Conversations like that allow me to lay the groundwork for others that may come up later in his life.

I try to teach him that sometimes hard things happen in life, and when they do it's normal to feel angry or sad, but there are ways to feel the emotions and then move on. You don't have to stay in a sad or angry place forever. I want him to know that the life he leads is more privileged in many ways than the lives of some of his friends, and that some people may see him differently because he's a white male. Above all, when he's older, I want him to understand consent.

I thought back recently to a conversation I had with my naturopath after he was born, when I was so distraught about not feeling a maternal bond with him and fearing I never would. She told me that she and her wife had two kids, and her wife had carried both pregnancies. She reminded me that same-sex mothers who don't carry the pregnancy also miss out on the oxytocin transfer. Yet, like fathers, they still feel an incredibly deep bond of love for their children. They feel that inviolate bond because they choose to love them.

I had no reason to believe her words at the time, but I clung to them, and once I was through the worst of the postpartum months, I didn't have to choose to love Kaden. I fell head over heels in love with him just like every other adoring parent on the planet falls in love with their kids. In my case, the falling-hard part just got delayed. I also clung to something Sandra said to me when we first started working together about how neuroplastic our brains are and how mine would continue to rewire and in time I would heal.

One of the ways I know how much Kaden has helped me heal is how I feel now when the anniversary of my attack looms. That date is burned into my memory. I think about it a lot, in the same way that I imagine anyone who has suffered a trauma or loss would think about the day it happened. Early on, people close to me sent me notes on the anniversary of that day to let me know they were thinking of me, the way you might send a note to someone who'd lost a loved one. I always mark the anniversary of the attack. In a way, it serves as a marker of how far I have come.

Before I had Kaden, every November when the anniversary approached, I was filled with dread. I always had to plan what

I was going to do on that day so it didn't rip me apart. I always knew when the anniversary was four days out, then three, then two. I still know when it's approaching every year, but now that Kaden is in my life, instead of fearing the day and dwelling on my pain, I get to spend it with him. And that is what I do. Every single anniversary since his birth, except the year of his birth, when he was in the NICU, I tuck him into bed, cuddle up with him and bask in the joy he brings me.

Besides Kaden, my life is filled with all the usual things that have always filled my cup: work, sports and travel, family and community. I now have a busy practice treating adolescents, young adults, middle-aged women and sexual assault survivors. I continue to hold a certain number of spots for lower-fee and pro bono work for the sexual assault survivors, as I promised myself I would. Just before the pandemic, I bought a house in a great neighbourhood with lots of families and kids for Kaden to play with, much like the neighbourhood where I grew up. During the pandemic, I had my garage converted into a therapy room. I love it, my clients love it, and I love that it's only steps from my home.

I'm not with anyone at the time of this writing. Cris and I broke up before the pandemic, but I think of her as my angel who came into my life and watched over me at the precise moment when I needed watching over the most. We remain family, and she is still a central figure in Kaden's life. Otherwise, I just keep putting one foot in front of the other the way I did after the tsunami, when I slid my feet into my flip-flops and kept on walking. I keep moving forward and into the future, whatever it may hold.

Acknowledgments

I would not be where I am today, nor would I have written this book, without the support of countless people.

First, I owe endless and unwavering gratitude to my family, who believed in my resilience when I had no reason to believe in it myself. To my parents I owe a particular debt of gratitude: You trusted me to find my way when the path I chose terrified you. You didn't just understand why I wanted to write this book—you are the reason it is a reality.

To my devoted village of friends and my angel, who showed up for me without question and helped me through my most despairing days, often pressing pause on your own lives to lift up mine: I will never forget your loving support.

To Wendy Dennis: Thank you for believing in my story and collaborating with me to help bring it to life. You made it so easy to share what was in my heart, saw the fortitude in my words—however quiet they were at times—and set them down beautifully on the page.

To the pioneers and experts whose work I have studied for years and who have been my teachers and guides throughout this journey: Bessel van der Kolk, Peter A. Levine, Russ Harris, Janina Fisher, Deb Dana, Pat Ogden, Dan Siegel, Kristin Neff, Judith Herman, Marsha M. Linehan and others. I haven't just drawn on your work extensively in my therapeutic practice to help others—it is largely because of what I learned from you that I was able to understand my own trauma and find my footing.

To the good men in this world, thank you for making a difference to those of us who need to be reminded of the goodness in men. We appreciate you more than you will ever know.

To the sexual assault survivors, wherever you are: I see you and want you to know that your fortitude and resilience are a constant inspiration to me. Thank you for giving me the courage to share my story.

A big thank-you to Girl Friday Productions for an enjoyable and collaborative first-time publishing experience.

Finally, to my son, Kaden, my heart: Your light brightens my life and fills my soul with love and joy, even in my darkest moments. You have always been, and continue to be, my greatest source of healing.

Strategies and Resources

BREATHWORK

When you're in a fight-or-flight state, using your breath to activate the vagus nerve and in turn the parasympathetic nervous system can be the quickest way to calm yourself down. Below are some examples of breathwork strategies I have found helpful. Find two or three that work for you and use them when you need to:

1. Box Breathing: Slowly inhale for four seconds, then hold your breath for four seconds. Exhale for four seconds, then hold your breath for another four seconds.
2. 2x Breathing: Slowly inhale for four seconds, then exhale for eight seconds.
3. 4-7-8 Breathing: Follow a cycle of inhaling for four seconds, holding your breath for seven seconds and exhaling for eight seconds.

Resources:

- www.everydayhealth.com/alternative-health /living-with/ways-practice-breath-focused -meditation
- https://health.clevelandclinic.org/breathwork

HUMMING

Humming can be helpful when you are feeling dysregulated or your sympathetic nervous system has been activated and you're in fight-or-flight mode. Humming creates a vibration on the vagus nerve, which in turn stimulates the parasympathetic nervous system to send you into a rest-and-relax state.

Resources:

- https://health.clevelandclinic.org/vagus-nerve -stimulation
- https://psychcentral.com/anxiety/vagus-nerve -cooling-anxiety

5-4-3-2-1 ORIENTING TO PRESENCE AND SAFETY

This exercise uses the five senses in a mindful way to orient your body to the present and to safety. Write your observations in the spaces provided below:

1. Acknowledge and name five things you see around you:
2. Acknowledge and name four things you can touch/feel around you:
3. Acknowledge and name three things you hear around you:
4. Acknowledge and name two things you can smell around you:
5. Acknowledge and name one thing you can taste:

Resources:

- www.calm.com/blog/5-4-3-2-1-a-simple-exercise
  -to-calm-the-mind#:~:text=The%2054321%20(or%
  205%2C%204,1%20thing%20you%20can%20taste
- www.choosingtherapy.com/54321-method
- www.positivepsychology.com/act-worksheets
- https://therapistaid.com/therapy-article
  /grounding-techniques-article
- www.traumaresearchuk.org/the-54321-grounding
  -technique
- www.urmc.rochester.edu/behavioral-health
  -partners/bhp-blog/april-2018/5-4-3-2-1-coping
  -technique-for-anxiety.aspx

TIPP

TIPP stands for temperature, intense exercise, paced breathing and paired muscle relaxation. Employ this strategy, which is a form of dialectical behaviour therapy (DBT), if you are having a panic attack.

> T: Temperature: To activate the vagus nerve and slow down your breathing and heart rate, splash cold water on your face, step into a cold shower or drink cold water.
>
> I: Intense Exercise: To expend the body's pent-up energy, do push-ups, do jumping jacks or go for a run.
>
> P: Paced Breathing: Use the breathwork examples above to slow down your breathing and activate your parasympathetic system.

P: Paired Muscle Relaxation: To calm yourself down, pair your breathing with relaxing your muscles by tensing your muscles and inhaling through your nostrils at the same time. Notice where you feel tension. As you exhale, think about the word *relax* as you relax your muscles and feel the tension release from your body.

Resources:

- www.dbt.tools
- www.dialecticalbehaviortherapy.com/distress-tolerance/tipp

LOWERING ANXIETY

When your body is in fight-or-flight mode due to a perceived threat, allow yourself to scan the environment and say out loud: "I notice I am feeling anxious. Thanks for trying to keep me safe, brain, but I am not in any danger right now."

Complete the following statement: I notice that I am feeling anxious. I notice I am having thoughts of _____ _____. Tell yourself: *Anxiety feels awful in my body, but it is not dangerous. It is just cortisol and adrenaline I am feeling, and the feeling will pass. I can use some of my strategies if I need to.*

Resources:

- www.actmindfully.com.au/wp-content/uploads /2019/08/ACT-Made-Simple-The-Extra-Bits-Russ -Harris-August-2019-Update.pdf
- www.thehappinesstrap.com/category/defusion
- www.youtube.com/watch?v=-bkD1kpv58k

DROPPING THE ANCHOR

This is a mindfulness technique used in acceptance and commitment therapy (ACT). It is designed to help you manage difficult feelings by grounding yourself in the present moment and is predicated on the idea that while storms—i.e., overwhelming experiences or emotions—can come and go, it is possible to remain anchored and strong amid them. The goal isn't to eliminate the sensation but rather to weather the storm, or distressful moment, by using your body and the present moment as an anchor.

1. Acknowledge the storm—i.e., the overwhelming experience or emotion, thoughts or body sensations you are experiencing—by finishing this sentence: I am feeling _____.
2. Choose an anchor, such as placing your feet on the floor. Push your feet into the floor, straighten your spine and notice the strength in your back.
3. While you are doing this exercise, engage some of your other senses. Notice your breath, your diaphragm expanding and contracting, your body

swaying from side to side. Roll your shoulders backwards and forwards.

4. Continue to do the breathing exercises mentioned above. While you are doing them, pay attention to what you see, hear and feel around you.

Resources:

- www.actmindfully.com.au/free-stuff/free-audio
- www.youtube.com/watch?v=4PDHxA4Fij4

RADICAL ACCEPTANCE

Radical acceptance, another DBT strategy, is predicated on the idea that some things are beyond your control and that continuing to struggle against them will lead only to greater suffering. It is about embracing the present moment—even deeply uncomfortable or painful moments—without trying to change or control them.

Here are some helpful coping statements that you can employ:

1. This is a moment of suffering, and it will pass.
2. I can control only the things that I can control.
3. I accept this moment as it is.
4. It is not helpful for me to try to change or fight the past.
5. May I forgive myself for not being perfect.

Resources:

- www.dbtselfhelp.com/radical-acceptance -turning-the-mind
- www.dialecticalbehaviortherapy.com/distress -tolerance/radical-acceptance
- www.self-compassion.org

GLIMMERS

This strategy, a component of polyvagal theory, uses micromoments to help with regulation and fosters a sense of well-being. Generally, these are moments of joy or peace that cue our nervous system that we are safe or calm. Examples of this could be watching a cute puppy play, hearing a familiar voice, seeing a rainbow or engaging in a random act of kindness.

How to use glimmers, a term and idea coined by Deb Dana, in your everyday life: Be aware of the things you notice around you that make you smile, bring you a moment of peace, make you laugh or feel familiar in a good way. Noticing these things cues your body to feel safe and keep you regulated.

Resources:

- www.mi-psych.com.au/understanding-your -window-of-tolerance
- www.nicabm.com/trauma-how-tohelp-your -clients-understand-their-window-oftolerance
- www.rhythmofregulation.com/glimmers

BOOKS I FOUND HELPFUL

First, We Make the Beast Beautiful: A New Journey Through Anxiety, Sarah Wilson, Dey Street Books, 2018

The Body Keeps the Score: Mind, Brain and Body in the Transformation of Trauma, Bessel van der Kolk, Penguin Books, 2015

Waking the Tiger: Healing Trauma, Peter A. Levine, North Atlantic Books, 1997

The Happiness Trap: How to Stop Struggling and Start Living, Russ Harris, Trumpeter, 2008

Self-Compassion: The Proven Power of Being Kind to Yourself, Kristin Neff, William Morrow Paperbacks, 2015

Trauma and Recovery: The Aftermath of Violence—From Domestic Abuse to Political Terror, Judith Herman, Basic Books, 1997

The Boy Who Was Raised as a Dog: And Other Stories from a Child Psychiatrist's Notebook—What Traumatized Children Can Teach Us About Loss, Love, and Healing, Bruce Perry and Maia Szalavitz, Basic Books, 2017

The Mindful Self-Compassion Workbook: A Proven Way to Accept Yourself, Build Inner Strength, and Thrive, Kristin Neff and Christopher Germer, Guilford Press, 2018

STRATEGIES I WANT
TO REMEMBER

_____

_____

_____

_____

_____

_____

_____

_____

_____

_____

_____

_____

_____

strategies i want to remember

ABOUT THE AUTHOR

© Nathalie Amlani, Pictonat Photography

Sara Davidson is a registered psychotherapist in private practice in Toronto. She is also a sexual assault survivor who fought relentlessly to reclaim her sense of safety and self in the face of unspeakable trauma. Formerly a secondary school teacher, semi-professional athlete and coach, she regularly speaks, consults and conducts workshops on gender-based violence for schools, non-profits and corporate audiences. Passionately committed to advocating for individuals who have experienced gender-based violence, especially working with adolescents and young adults around issues of consent, resilience and forgiveness, she brings the unique perspective of a survivor, psychotherapist and mentor to the task.

www.ingramcontent.com/pod-product-compliance
Lightning Source LLC
Chambersburg PA
CBHW030920140626
46545CB00016B/2192